Material and Spiritual Prosperity for God's End Time People

A. DODRIDGE BOWERS

The righteous shall flourish like the palm tree:

he shall grow like a cedar in Lebanon.

Those that be planted in the house of the LORD shall flourish in the courts of our God.

They shall still bring forth fruit in old age; they shall be fat and flourishing.

(Psalm 92:12-14)

Copyright © 2024 A. Dodridge Bowers. All rights reserved.

All rights reserved. No portion of this book may be reproduced, stored in a retrieval system, or transmitted in any form or by any means – electronic, mechanical, photocopy, recording, scanning, or other – except for a brief quotation in critical reviews or articles, without the prior written permission of the publisher or author.

Unless otherwise noted, all scriptures are from the KING JAMES VERSION, public domain.

Published by:

Great-Nest Publishing Inc.

Cover designed by Calbert Simpson

Dedication and Acknowledgement

This book is dedicated to the memory of Hildred Nerissa Bowers, the woman who brought me into the world and mothered and fathered me spiritually. She brought me into the Seventh-day Adventist Church at the tender age of two and, by precept and example, nurtured me until I made my own decision to accept Jesus Christ as my Lord and Saviour. Early in my life, she taught me the principles of faithful stewardship, which was the initial inspiration for this book.

I also dedicate it to the memory of Alpheus Augustus Bowers, my father, who, though he was not a Christian, was a strict father who did what he could to shield me from activities that destroyed other young men in the rural community in which I grew up.

I must also mention my three sisters, Jascinth, Glenda, and Elaine, who encouraged and supported me financially when I accepted God's call to pastoral ministry.

My wife Winsome, of over forty-one years, and the two children, Jody-Ann and Garland, whom we brought into this world, have been an inspiration and a tower of strength. I cannot claim to have been the best husband and father, but they have tolerated and embraced me as I executed the ministry that God gave me. I am looking forward to continuing to share life with them in God's soon-coming kingdom.

Finally, I express heartfelt gratitude to those of my ministerial friends and faithful laymen and women who believed in me and stood with me through good and bad times. You are too numerous to mention, but heaven knows and will reward you adequately.

Table of Contents

Dedication and Acknowledgement...4

Introduction..8

Chapter 1: God's Plan for His People 10

Chapter 2: Fullness of Life for Believers...............................13

Chapter 3: Successful Living 17

Chapter 4: Progressive Living 26

Chapter 5: Loving as Jesus Loves..32

Chapter 6: Amazing Faith 39

Chapter 7: Christians and Money 46

Chapter 8: Living For the Glory of the Lord 55

Chapter 9: Being Extravagant for Jesus..................................63

Chapter 10: Thanksgiving and Living 69

Chapter 11: Giving and Living 77

Chapter 12: The Joys and Blessings of Obedience 84

Chapter 13: Worshipping in Spirit and in Truth 89

Chapter 14: Succeeding in Difficult Times 94

Chapter 15: God's Prosperity Program 101

Chapter 16: Laying up Treasures in Heaven 107

Chapter 17: Facing the End Time Financial Challenges 113

Chapter 18: Rejoicing in Tribulation 121

Chapter 19: Aids For Attaining Fullness of Life 126

Chapter 20: Those Who Will Hear The "Well Done" 134

About the Author 140

Introduction

A critical aspect of God's plan for human redemption is the repopulation of heaven and the New Earth with beings who have accepted Jesus Christ as Lord and Saviour. However, those who are so privileged will have to experience a total transformation in every aspect of life. This level of development, which I refer to as the "Fullness of Life," can only be achieved by God's grace and power.

God has made provision that anyone and everyone who desires to obtain this goal may achieve it, and He has given us a program called Christian Stewardship. It requires us to manage every aspect of our lives, following principles laid down by Christ Himself.

This book, *Fullness of Life for Believers*, discusses principles from the Bible and Ellen White's writings. It is arranged with relevant passages and quotations to challenge and inspire readers. It examines the way we worship and work, make and spend money, and relate to hardships and trials. It also helps us understand what true success is and how to achieve it. The coming time of trouble is also discussed, highlighting how we may develop the faith to endure to the end.

Chapter 1

God's Plan for His People

"For I know the thoughts that I think toward you, saith the Lord, thoughts of peace, and not of evil, to give you an expected end" (Jeremiah 29:11). These words declare that our loving heavenly Father has an excellent plan for a future for all His children.

From the creation of Adam and Eve in Eden to the restoration of man in the New Earth, as outlined in the last chapter of the book of Revelation, God's plan for man has always been a glorious one. It was His original intention that human beings would enjoy a world full of peace, love, and plenty and free of sin and suffering. Even after sin intruded, He still intended to achieve His original desire, so He promised a Redeemer (*Genesis* 3:15).

As a part of His program for man's restoration to the original ideal, He chose Abraham and his descendants to be His goodwill ambassadors. Egyptian bondage for over four hundred years seemed to have thwarted the plan. However, after their miraculous deliverance, followed by their turbulent wilderness wandering, Moses, in his farewell address to them, reiterated Jehovah's plan of conditional prosperity. After repeated failures and warnings of Babylonian captivity, through Jeremiah, the Lord made it clear that He did not abandon His plan. He still desired to bless and prosper His people (Jeremiah 29:11).

David, who led God's people to unprecedented levels of national success and prestige militarily, materially, and spiritually, confidently expressed that God would show him the path to life (*Psalm* 16:11). After praising the Lord in Psalm 34, he sets out God's plan for a successful life. By the time Jesus appeared on earth, the chosen people, like the rest of the world, had reached unprecedented moral and spiritual degradation, yet Jesus declared, "I am come that they might have life, and that they might have it more abundantly" (*John* 10:10).

The Apostle John, in his third epistle, under inspiration, expressed his supreme wish that the brethren would prosper and be in health, even as their souls prosper (3 John 2). Also, in his masterpiece, the Book of Revelation, which sets out the end-time experience of God's people, he begins by praising Jesus for making us kings and priests (Revelation 1:6).

It has never been God's idea that His people should live in a world of sin and suffering. Even when and where He allows it, it is to discipline the people and influence them to choose the road leading them back to abundant living here on earth and ultimately to eternal life in His everlasting kingdom (*Matthew 7:13-14*).

QUESTIONS FOR CONTEMPLATION

1. Has God always had a plan for man's well-being?

2. Why does God allow suffering sometimes?

3. As outlined in 3 John 2, what are the areas of prosperity that God wishes for us?

Chapter 2

Fullness of Life for Believers

Saul of Tarsus was one of the fiercest persecutors of the Christian church. It was the mission of his life to destroy it. However, from a destroyer, he became a builder. He experienced the most dramatic conversion and transformation after encountering Jesus on the Damascus Road while he was on a mission to root out the members of the hated Christian community that dwelt in that city. He also received a change of name, indicative of his new status.

Paul immersed himself fully in his new-found faith and distinguished himself by his devotion to Jesus, whom he discovered was the promised Messiah of Old Testament prophesies. His commitment to Christ is expressed in his famous words, "For me to live is Christ, and to die is gain" (*Philippians*

1:21). In the same book, chapter three, He outlines how he rejected all his worldly positions and achievements to win Christ.

Paul experienced the Gospel's full power and wanted believers to have the same. He expresses this in his prayer set out in his letter to the brethren at Ephesus: "For this cause I bow my knees unto the Father of our Lord Jesus Christ, Of whom the whole family in heaven and earth is named, That he would grant you, according to the riches of his glory, to be strengthened with might by his Spirit in the inner man; That Christ may dwell in your hearts by faith; that ye, being rooted and grounded in love, May be able to comprehend with all saints what is the breadth, and length, and depth, and height; And to know the love of Christ, which passeth knowledge, that ye might be filled with all the fulness of God" (*Ephesians* 3: 14-19). Since we are God's children, His qualities should be replicated in our lives; hence, the title of this book, ***Fullness of Life for Believers.***

The Christian life is elevating. John expresses it very well when he writes, "And from Jesus Christ, who is the faithful witness, and the first begotten of the dead, and the prince of the kings of the earth. Unto him that loved us and washed us from our sins in his own blood, and hath made us kings and priests unto God and his Father" (Revelation 1:5-6).

Here is a summary of what is contained in this fullness of life that Paul asked the Lord to grant us:

- We manifest strong faith a deep commitment to Christ.

- We receive and share His love.

- We gladly obey and serve Him.

- Our lives are joyfully worshipping Him, and we live for the honor and glory of His name.

- Also, we place God's business first, seek to please Him in all things, and exhibit unshakable faith. This is the most rewarding kind of living.

Another manifestation of this fullness in life is that we are constantly growing because we have not yet become perfect. Jesus holds up before us the goal that He has set for us: "Be ye therefore perfect, even as your Father which is in heaven is perfect" (Matthew 5:48). When we reach that goal of this fullness of life, then we will be ready to spend eternity with Him in heaven and the New Earth. We must remember this as we live each day and keep pressing on the upward way, gaining new heights each day.

QUESTIONS FOR CONTEMPLATION

1. Can you think of Bible characters you think experienced fullness of life? Name one.

2. Which aspects of the fullness of life are you now enjoying?

3. What do you think will happen to you if you do not experience fullness of

4. life before Jesus' return?

5. If you are alive at Jesus' return, do you think you will be a part of the 144,000 group?

Chapter 3

Successful Living

God wants His people to succeed in every legitimate pursuit of life, and He has made provision for us to achieve this success. Those who are truly successful in life are the ones who experience fullness of life—the abundant life that Jesus said He came to facilitate.

Moses, in his farewell address to the Israelites, challenged them to "Keep therefore the words of this covenant, and do them, that he may prosper in all that ye do"(Deuteronomy 29:9). The Apostle John wished above all things that believers may "prosper and be in health, even as thy soul prospereth"(3 John 2). And it is important to remember that God's way always leads to success.

In talking about success, we should remember that God views success differently from the world, in as much as His ways are higher than ours, and that He takes an eternal perspective of life.

Sometimes, when we think we are failing, God might regard us as succeeding or being prepared for success! Take the examples of Joseph and Moses. Joseph, as a slave in Egypt, and Moses, in the wilderness tending sheep, might have been regarded as miserable failures. However, from prison, Joseph rose to the pinnacle of power in Egypt (Genesis 37-50), and Moses became one of the most outstanding leaders the world has ever seen (Hebrews 11:24-28).

On the other hand, the Apostle Paul, at a point in his life, believed he was enjoying supreme success. After meeting the exalted Jesus, he suddenly recognized the worthlessness of the life he was pursuing and abandoned his position, status, and privileges to become a devoted follower of Christ (Philippians 3:4-7). All three men appreciated that true success includes life's spiritual and eternal dimensions.

Principles that Ensure Success

Certain principles must be followed for us to be truly successful. Our all-wise, loving Heavenly Father has laid down these principles, and those who have followed them have never been disappointed. These directives guarantee a satisfying life on earth and eternal life in God's kingdom.

Principle 1: Recognition of God

David wrote, "The fear of the Lord is the beginning of wisdom: a good understanding have all they that do his commandments" (Psalm 111:10). This means that God must be acknowledged and served for who He is—Creator, Sustainer, and Redeemer. Ellen White counsels, "Young friends, the fear of the Lord lies at the very foundation of all progress; it is the beginning of wisdom. Your heavenly Father has claims upon you; for without solicitation or merit on your part He gives you the bounties of His providence; and more than this, He has given you all heaven in one gift, that of His beloved Son. In return for this infinite gift, He claims of you willing obedience" (Messages to Young People, p. 39). A life that is lived independent of God ultimately results in disaster.

Principle 2: Embracing God's Will

This second principle is closely related to the first. Anyone who recognizes God will embrace His will and do so joyfully. When on earth, Jesus, our Savior, lived by His Father's will. His followers will do the same. David asserted in Psalm 16:11, "Thou wilt shew me the path of life: in thy presence is fulness of joy; at thy right hand there are pleasures for evermore." Also, Ellen White sets out this challenge for the youth, "God asks us to be true to Him...His will must be made our will in all things. Any departure from this standard degrades our moral nature. It may result in lifting us, in enriching us, and in seating us beside princes; but in the eyes of God, we are unclean and unholy. We have sold our birthright for selfish interest and gain, and in the books of heaven it is written of us, weighed in the balances of the sanctuary, and found wanting" (Signs of the Times, Jan. 21, 1897).

Principle 3: Diligence and Regularity

True success does not come by chance or accident. We must take deliberate steps to achieve such; hard work and regular habits are integral to this process. The Bible challenges us to learn from the ant. Her achievement, considering her size, can teach us valuable lessons. God will not reward laziness and idleness, and Ellen White counsels us that "Men and women of God must be diligent in study, earnest in the acquirement of knowledge, never wasting an hour. Through persevering exertion, they may rise to almost any degree of eminence as Christians, as people of power and influence (*Gospel Workers*, p. 278).

It is also essential that we be regular and systematic in our habits. Haphazard approaches will not position us to do our best. As people of God, we should note that "people of business can be truly successful only by having regular hours for rising, for prayer, for meals, and for retiring" (ibid). If this is so in business, how much more important is it in the spiritual realm?

Principle 4: Economy

From Jesus's example of feeding the five thousand, we learn that waste and extravagance should not be tolerated in the Christian experience. Jesus instructed His disciples to "gather up the fragments that remain, that nothing be lost"(John 6:12), even though everyone was already well-fed.

Principle 5: Liberality

A very indispensable principle of success in life's material and spiritual areas is kindness and sharing with God and others. Solomon observed, "There is that scattereth, and yet increaseth; and there is that withholdeth more than is meet, but it tendeth to poverty. The liberal soul shall be made fat: and he that watereth shall be watered also himself" (Proverbs 11:24-25). Ellen White encouraged liberality, suggesting it would undoubtedly result in prosperity (Ministry of Healing, p.187). And we should never forget the admonition of Jesus when He said, "Give and it shall be given unto you…"(Luke 6:38). So, it is in our interest to return to the Lord and share with others. It will go a long way in enhancing our material and eternal success.

How the Bible Views Success

God is deeply interested in the success of His people. He wants us to understand the nature of real success, and He wants us to experience it. Therefore, it is quite understandable that the subject is addressed by many of the writers of the Bible.

On a Sabbath day in church, Jesus warned the congregation against covetousness after a young man asked His assistance in securing some of his dead father's possessions from his selfish brother. He then warned the people that "...a man's life consisteth not in the abundance of the things which he possesseth (Luke 12:15-21). For Jesus, having a great amount of material possessions does not indicate that that person is necessarily successful. Real success for Jesus includes being rich toward God. Success that is merely material makes one a fool. That's why Jesus warned about the deceitfulness of riches on another occasion and cautioned that "...a rich man shall hardly enter into the kingdom of heaven" (Matthew 19:23). And to all of us, He asks the question, "For what shall it profit a man, if he gain the whole world, and lose his own soul?" (Mark 8:36). That certainly is not success, but disaster!

Reference has already been made to the Apostle Paul, who, having come to understand real success, turned his back on his wealth and position in the Jewish economy. He advises us to shun the company of those who believe that "gain is godliness" and confronts us with the idea that "godliness with contentment is great gain." Paul also warned that those pursuing riches "will fall into temptation and a snare, and into many foolish and hurtful lusts, which drown men in destruction and perdition." So, for him, success means fighting the good fight of faith and laying hold on eternal life (1 Timothy 6:12).

Evidence of True Success

People in different sectors of society view success in variable ways. For the athlete, it is amassing gold medals and titles; for the politician, it is attaining power and holding on to it; for the entertainer, it is fame and the following of fans; and for the businessman, it is amassing wealth. While the above have their places in the scheme of things, they are limited and inadequate to define success. For the Christian, success transcends materialism and all the world's accolades.

Wealth is not a good measure of success because it fails from time to time in different ways. So, there is no security in anything human or earthly. That's why Jesus has admonished us, "Sell that ye have, and give alms; provide yourselves bags which wax not old, a treasure in the heavens that faileth not, where no thief approacheth, neither moth corrupteth" (*Luke* 12:33). There is also another insidious danger from wealth; it tends to blind the eyes of its possessor to the real thing. As Ellen White puts it, "Hoarded wealth is not merely useless, it is a curse. In this life, it is a snare to the soul, drawing the affections away from the heavenly treasure" (Christ Object Lessons, p. 352). She also warned that "Hoarded wealth will soon be worthless. When the decree shall go forth that none shall buy or sell except they have the mark of the beast, very much means will be of no avail" (*Last Day Events*, p. 148).

For Paul, success is "godliness with contentment"(1 Timothy 6:6). For Solomon, it is having "little with the fear of the Lord" (Proverbs 15:16). That's why he wrote, "Give me neither poverty nor riches; feed me with food convenient for me" (Proverbs 30:8). And one man has said, "Success is having what you need when you need it."

Ultimately, the proof of real success is what happens to us at the end of this world. If, by God's grace, we are privileged to hear from the lips of Jesus, "Well done, thou good and faithful servant: thou hast been faithful over a few things, I will make thee ruler over many things: enter thou into the joy of thy lord" (Matthew 25:21), then we know we would have achieved real and lasting success in life.

QUESTIONS FOR CONTEMPLATION

1. Is God interested in the material prosperity of His people?

2. What are the elements of a successful life from the Bible's perspective?

3. Why is money not a good measure of a successful life?

4. What are some of the dangers of hoarded wealth?

5. What are some of the problems with the marks of success from the world's view?

6. What is the ultimate proof of real success in life?

Chapter 4

Progressive Living

"But the path of the just is as the shining light, that shineth more and more unto the perfect day."
(Proverbs 4:18)

The fullness of life that Jesus has promised includes continuous growth. Therefore, one identifying mark of a sincere Christian is an improving experience, physically, mentally, materially, and spiritually. All living things grow, and anything that is not growing dies. In other words, each day, we should improve at living. Solomon had that in mind when he wrote the passage quoted above.

Peter encourages and challenges us to " grow in grace, and in the knowledge of our Lord and Saviour Jesus Christ" (2 Peter 3:18). He also describes the process and method of this growth when he wrote, "And beside this, giving all diligence, add to your faith virtue; and to virtue knowledge; And to knowledge temperance; and to temperance patience; and to patience godliness; And to godliness brotherly kindness; and to brotherly kindness charity" (2 Peter 1:5-7).

We are to examine our lives through the eye of the Spirit, discover our deficiencies, and seek to develop these Christlike graces. Ellen White says that while we are working on the plan of addition, Christ will work on the plan of multiplication (Acts of the Apostles, p. 532). Also, Peter asserts that "…if these things be in you, and abound, they make you that ye shall neither be barren nor unfruitful in the knowledge of our Lord Jesus Christ" (2 Peter 1:8). Ellen White endorses the point by stating that "there is no possibility of failure before the one who, advancing by faith, ascends round by round, ever upward and onward, to the topmost round of the ladder that reaches even to the portals of heaven" (Ibid).

The life of Jesus on earth was a clear and powerful demonstration of progressive living. Luke records that "Jesus increased in wisdom and stature, and in favour with God and man" (Luke 2:52). He experienced mental, physical, social, and spiritual development. So, Jesus's life was one of continual advancement, and He is our example in all things.

Provisions for Our Development

Jesus does not only expect us to grow; He has made provision for every human being to grow. Three primary factors are common to all humanity. God has given everyone a mind, the same amount of time, and some talents; when these are rightly used, life will improve.

The *mind* is the most powerful faculty in human beings and is the governing element in every life. More than anything else, it determines the outcome of every person. Solomon advises, "Keep thy heart(mind) with all diligence, for out of it are the issues of life" (Proverbs 4:23). He further cautions, "...as he thinketh in his heart, so is he"(Proverbs 23:7), and one philosopher has said that "The mind is the measure of the man." These statements challenge us to guard our minds carefully and use them well because they ultimately determine our destiny. So, we are to think big and aim high, for we are what we think.

Life is lived in time. God has given us the same amount of this commodity, but our use of it makes the difference. Some people complain about not having enough time, but this is untrue. The problem is how they use it. Our use of time may influence the length and quality of our lives. That's why Solomon informs us that "To every thing there is a season, and a time to every purpose under the heaven: A time to be born, and a time to die; a time to plant, and a time to pluck up that which is planted; A time to kill, and a time to heal; a time to break down, and a time to build up..." (Ecclesiastes 3:1-8).

There is a massive misuse of time in our world. Some people work when they should be sleeping, while some sleep when they should be working, and there is much idleness. Some students play when they should study, and vice-versa. Ellen White reminds us that "Our time belongs to God. Every moment is His, and we are under the most solemn obligation to improve it to His glory. Of no talent He has given will He require a more strict account than of our time" (Christ's Object Lessons, p. 342).

Time squandered can never be regained, so we are to make the best use of every moment of every day. This will facilitate our advancement in life.

The talents in the story in Matthew 25 are units of money distributed to the lord's servants. They may also represent the abilities the Lord Jesus allocates to His children to carry forward His work. Whatever application is used, the fact is that everyone has been entrusted with the gift of life and should labor to improve his lot. God expects us to improve, and if we thankfully manage His blessings carefully, our lives will experience growth, spiritually and otherwise. Christians are especially under obligation to work for this progress, as Ellen White stated when she wrote, "Of every Christian, the Lord requires growth in efficiency and capability in every line" (Ibid, 331).

The one-talent man manifested ingratitude, regarded his lord as demanding and unreasonable, and did not put his talent to use. People who regard God as unreasonable in His directives and requirements usually make no meaningful progress in life. The words of Ellen White are full of instruction: "God will accept only those who are determined to aim high. He places every human agent under obligation to do his best"(*Ibid*).

The story of the talents also teaches us about the importance of service in a progressive life. The servant who received one talent but refused to serve his lord even though he had something to work with robbed him of a profound blessing. When we serve, we bless others, but we also bless ourselves. Solomon reminds us that "The liberal soul shall be made fat: and he that watereth shall be watered also himself" (Proverbs 11:25), and Ellen White outlines a beautiful presentation of the same principle by stating that "Service, while making us a blessing to others, brings great blessing to ourselves." For her, unselfishness underlies all true development "because through unselfish service, we receive the highest culture of every faculty" (Education, p. 16). So, those who want to enhance their lives should seize every opportunity to serve others.

QUESTIONS FOR CONTEMPLATION

1. Apart from the principles listed above, what other factors are there that may contribute to improvement in our lives?

2. Why is it important that we aim for improvement in our lives?

3. Can you think of other Bible passages that speak about making progress in life? List them.

4. Have your life improved since you became a Christian?

5. Do you think we will continue to make progress in life in the kingdom?

Chapter 5

Loving as Jesus Loves

God's most important attribute is love, and the greatest demonstration of His love is that He sent His only Son to die for our sins (John 3:16). All of God's other attributes and actions towards us result from His love, and He always works for our good.

Christians are expected and required to emulate God's love in their lives, and to do so, we must understand the nature of God's love, the essence of it, and how it operates. As part of his explanation of being filled with all the fullness of God, Paul prays "that Christ may dwell in your hearts by faith; that ye, being rooted and grounded in love, May be able to comprehend with all saints what is the breadth, and length, and depth, and height; And to know the love of Christ, which passeth knowledge, that ye might be filled with all the fulness of God" (*Ephesians* 3:17-

19). We must understand God's love to correctly display it before the world.

The Bible teaches that God loves the world (John 3:16), including good and bad people, those who serve Him, and those who do not. As the beloved apostle explains in His letter, we do not have to love God for Him to love us. He says, "Herein is love, not that we loved God, but that he loved us, and sent his Son to be the propitiation for our sins." When God first manifested His love to us, it was not because we showed Him love.

In Romans chapter five, Paul outlines a broader scope of God's love when he states, "For scarcely for a righteous man will one die: yet peradventure for a good man some would even dare to die. But God commendeth his love toward us, in that, while we were yet sinners, Christ died for us... For if, when we were enemies, we were reconciled to God by the death of his Son, much more, being reconciled, we shall be saved by his life" (Romans 5:7-10). This means that God loves sinners, and He even loves those sinners who go a step further to make themselves His enemies, like those Jewish leaders who crucified Jesus.

The love that God has for us is unconditional and unselfish. It does not depend on anything about us. That is why it is directed even towards sinners so that God's rain and sun benefit the just and the unjust alike. Even when our conduct does not please God, He still loves us. If love depends on the condition of the person it is directed to, it would be like and not love. Also, God does not manifest His love because He wants anything from us; He loves us to bless us because His love is not self-serving.

The same apostle John understood this concept well when he wrote, "In this was manifested the love of God toward us, because that God sent his only begotten Son into the world, that we might live through him" (1 John 4:9). God's love causes us to always act for the good of people. It is because of His love that some persons will suffer eternal destruction! This is the quality of the love He wants us to have for one another–love that seeks their good.

In Old Testament times, and early in the earthly ministry of Jesus, God's people were taught to love their neighbor as themselves *(Matthew* 22: 38-39), but later, Jesus introduced a new standard of measuring our love when He instructed His followers to "love one another, as I have loved you" *(John* 15:12). Maybe this is because most of us do not even love ourselves, or because we may not know what love is. Another reason is that we often mistake feelings for love, giving, or withholding good from others because of how we feel about them.

Once we come to know God, we are confronted by His love and inspired to emulate this love. The apostle John summarizes it beautifully: "Beloved, let us love one another: for love is of God; and everyone that loveth is born of God, and knoweth God. He that loveth not knoweth not God; for God is love." (*1 John* 4:7-8). Interestingly, Jesus declared that it is the practice of love that would identify individuals as His followers when He declared to His disciples, "A new commandment I give unto you, that ye love one another; as I have loved you, that ye also love one another. By this shall all men know that ye are my disciples, if ye have love one to another" (John 13: 34-35).

When we love others as Jesus loves us, it inspires us to act differently from others, even loving our enemies, the unloving and the unlovable. Christ teaches, "Ye have heard that it hath been said, thou shalt love thy neighbour, and hate thine enemy. But I say unto you, Love your enemies, bless them that curse you, do good to them that hate you, and pray for them which despitefully use you, and persecute you; That ye may be the children of your Father which is in heaven: for he maketh his sun to rise on the evil and on the good, and sendeth rain on the just and on the unjust. For if ye love them which love you, what reward have ye? do not even the publicans the same?" (*Matthew* 5:43-46).

Pay careful attention to the following insightful statements from Ellen White. They show that she had a great understanding of the essence of God's love and how we should reflect that love in our own lives:

"Christianity is the revealing of the tenderest affection for one another... Christ is to receive supreme love from the beings He has created. And He requires also that man shall cherish a sacred regard for his fellow beings. Every soul saved will be saved through love, which begins with God. True conversion is a change from selfishness to sanctified affection for God and for one another" (Selected Messages 1:114). Therefore, if we do not show this kind of love to others, we are not experiencing true Christianity, regardless of our profession.

"The attributes which God prizes most are charity and purity. These attributes should be cherished by every Christian" (*Testimonies for the Church* 5:85). Let us ardently and prayerfully seek to develop these attributes. They are more critical than many other things that we passionately pursue.

"The strongest argument in favour of the gospel is a loving and lovable Christian" (*The Ministry of Healing*, 470). Such a person will be more effective in doing evangelistic work.

"'Let us not love in word,' the apostle writes, 'but in deed and in truth.' The completeness of Christian character is attained when the impulse to help and bless others springs constantly from within. It is the atmosphere of this love surrounding the soul of the believer that makes him a savour of life unto life and enables God to bless his work. Supreme love for God and unselfish love for one another—this is the best gift that our heavenly Father can bestow. This love is not an impulse, but a divine principle, a permanent power. The unconsecrated heart cannot originate or produce it. Only in the heart where Jesus reigns is it found.

"We love Him, because He first loved us." Love is the ruling principle of action in the heart, renewed by divine grace. It modifies the character, governs the impulses, controls the passions, and ennobles the affections. This love, cherished in the soul, sweetens the life, and sheds a refining influence on all around. John strove to lead the believers to understand the exalted privileges that would come to them through the exercise of the spirit of love. This redeeming power, filling the heart, would control every other motive and raise its possessors above the corrupting influences of the world. And as this love was allowed full sway and became the motive power in the life, their trust and confidence in God and His dealing with them would be complete. They could then come to Him in full confidence of faith, knowing that they would receive from Him everything needful for their present and eternal good. "Herein is our love made perfect," he wrote, "that we may have boldness in the day of judgment: because as He is, so are we in this world." (*Acts of the Apostles*, 551).

From the above quotation, we should learn the following lessons: (1) As individuals and as a church community, we must spend more time and resources caring for others. (2) Love is not a feeling or a fleeting emotion. It is a principle that constantly guides our lives, influencing us to do good to others in need, whatever their situation. (3) The practice of true love is an essential part of the experience of fullness of life in the believer's development toward "the completeness of Christian character" which is an essential aspect of our readiness for heaven. May the Lord grant us grace to reach that level quickly.

QUESTIONS FOR CONTEMPLATION

1. Do you understand how much God loves you?
2. Do you love some persons more than you love others now?
3. Do you think God loves some other persons more than He loves you?
4. Do you believe that we will demonstrate different levels of love for different individuals in heaven?
5. How loving are you?
6. What percentage of your resources do you devote to helping others?

Chapter 6

Amazing Faith

One of the most important characteristics in the life of an individual experiencing fullness of life, the abundant life which Christ promised believers, is faith. To show its importance, the Bible says without it, it is impossible to please God! And Jesus says that if our faith is as small as a grain of mustard seed, we will be able to accomplish seemingly impossible feats.

In Hebrews chapter eleven, there is a list of persons who carried out some unbelievable things. Their faith made them look crazy in the eyes of others. Think of Abram, who, at the command of God, left his homeland without knowing where God was sending him and then later traveled a long journey to offer his only son as a sacrifice to the same God who before had forbidden child sacrifices! Think of Moses, who turned his back on the throne and the glories of Egypt to wander in the wilderness for forty years, after which he was given the responsibility to be the leader of the people of his nation who made his life so difficult. Think about Daniel and his three friends who defied the laws of Kings Darius and Nebuchadnezzar to obey God's laws, knowing that it could have led to their instant horrible death. Think of Esther, who risked her life to save her countrymen in Persia even though she was the queen of the kingdom.

As God's people in these last days, we must be prepared to develop and manifest this kind of faith if we expect to join them as the redeemed gather in the New Jerusalem to celebrate victory with Jesus and angels on that grand reunion day. Ellen White underscored the importance of possessing this extraordinary end-time faith when she wrote, "The season of distress and anguish before us will require a faith that can endure weariness, delay, and hunger—a faith that will not faint, though severely tried" (Great Controversy, 621). Having faith in God means that we trust His wisdom, power, and love. He is too wise to make mistakes when dealing with us and knows what is best for us. He has all the power to do what He wants for us, and He is too loving to fail us. If we do not develop that faith, we will be unfit to spend eternity with Him.

That coming "season of distress" will be an extremely difficult time for God's remnant people. It will be a time of severe testing of our characters to determine the spiritual material we are made of. "The assaults of Satan are fierce and determined, his delusions are terrible, but the Lord's eye is upon his people, and his ear listens to their cries. Their affliction is great, the flames of the furnace seem about to consume them; but the Refiner will bring them forth as gold tried in the fire" (*Ibid*). According to John, the author of the book of Revelation, God's people will face an economic boycott, and they will be threatened with death. All their civil and religious liberties will be taken away, and they will be regarded as the cause of all the troubles that will be on the nations at that time.

The main reason these trials will descend upon us is because of our determination to stand up for God and His word, especially the fourth commandment, which requires us to embrace the seventh day of the week as the Sabbath of Jehovah. So, we can imagine that the people will regard us as naïve and will ridicule us for allowing ourselves to suffer such terrible things just because of a day of worship. Will we be able to stand tall for God and His truth as Shadrach, Meshach, and Abednego did when they faced a similar situation? God will be looking for us to stand because it will be the final showdown between Christ and Satan, truth and error, good and evil. Also, the outcome will determine our eternal destiny.

For us to stand then, we must learn from now to develop that extraordinary faith in our daily lives. This faith is a part of the fullness of God that Paul prays for us in the third chapter of the book of Ephesians. When we have it, we will be able to say like the patriarch Job, "Though He slay me, yet will I trust Him" (*Job* 13:15). Interestingly, Ellen White advises us that "The period of probation is granted to all to prepare for that time." She says, "Jacob prevailed because he was persevering and determined. His victory is an evidence of the power of importunate prayer. All who will lay hold of God's promises, as he did, and be as earnest and persevering as he was, will succeed as he succeeded." (GC88 621).

Unfortunately, many people are not willing to face the challenges that are necessary for the development of this faith, so here is a statement to inspire us:

"The 'time of trouble such as never was,' is soon to open upon us; and we shall need an experience which we do not now possess, and which many are too indolent to obtain. It is often the case that trouble is greater in anticipation than in reality, but this is not true of the crisis before us. The most vivid presentation cannot reach the magnitude of the ordeal. In that time of trial, every soul must stand for himself before God" (GC88 622).

Here is another warning from Ellen White: "Those who are unwilling to deny self, to agonize before God, to pray long and earnestly for His blessing, will not obtain it. Wrestling with

God—how few know what it is! How few have ever had their souls drawn out after God with intensity of desire until every power is on the stretch. When waves of despair which no language can express sweep over the suppliant, how few cling with unyielding faith to the promises of God" (GC88 621.2). So, let us examine ourselves to determine our present situation and discover the adjustments we need to make to acquire this faith.

Also, she provides some encouragement: "God's love for His children during the period of their severest trial is as strong and tender as in the days of their sunniest prosperity; but it is needful for them to be placed in the furnace fire; their earthliness must be consumed that the image of Christ may be perfectly reflected" (*Idem*). This means that the end-time trials we will face will be for our good. They will assist in completing the work of transformation that we need to make us fit to dwell with Christ forever. Therefore, with gratitude, we should learn to trust God before that time comes. She also says, "Those who exercise but little faith now are in the greatest danger of falling under the power of Satanic delusions and the decree to compel the conscience. And even if they endure the test, they will be plunged into deeper distress and anguish in the time of trouble, because they have never made it a habit to trust in God. The lessons of faith which they have neglected, they will be forced to learn under a terrible pressure of discouragement" (*Idem*).

Developing faith in preparation for the coming time of trouble is so crucial that Ellen White insists, encourages, and suggests a way to approach the challenge: "We should now acquaint ourselves with God by proving his promises. Angels record every prayer that is earnest and sincere. We should rather dispense with selfish gratifications than neglect communion with God. The deepest poverty, the greatest self-denial, with His approval, is better than riches, honors, ease, and friendship without it. We must take time to pray. If we allow our minds to be absorbed by worldly interests, the Lord may give us time by removing from us our idols of gold, of houses, or of fertile lands" (GC88 622).

Our faith will be more than adequately rewarded; there is a glorious future awaiting us. Therefore, let us learn to trust God as we relate to all the issues that confront us in our daily lives so that we will come off as more than conquerors through Him who loves us.

QUESTIONS FOR CONTEMPLATION

1. How strong is your faith right now?

2. Have you reached the level of faith where you can say like Job, "Though He slay me, yet will I trust Him?"

3. Are you prepared, if it should become necessary, to walk away from all your possessions to maintain your loyalty to God?

4. Do you sometimes ask God why He allows certain difficulties to come upon you?

5. Would you be prepared to die for Christ in the coming "Time of Trouble?"

Chapter 7

Christians and Money

Money has always been a challenge for God's people. Some seem to have too much, while others think they don't have enough. Some are extravagant in spending, while others are penury, especially when it comes to supporting charity and the work of the Lord. Another problem associated with money is that many people think that having a significant amount of money and material possessions is evidence that the individual is having a good life. According to the Bible, money has proved to be a challenge for people in general in the last days. Therefore, Christians must learn to develop the right attitude and take the right approach to this crucial matter.

The Bible has much to say about money. Money, or material possessions, occupied a significant portion of Jesus' teachings and was central in most of His parables. Among other statements, Solomon says that "money answereth all things" and that it "is a defense" (Ecclesiastes 10:19, 7:12). Many other Bible writers address this vital area of life in one way or another.

Many people have an insatiable appetite for money, but the Bible warns against this attitude. In His parable of the *Rich Fool*, Jesus said, "Take heed, and beware of covetousness: for a man's life consisteth not in the abundance of the things which he possesseth" (Luke 12:15). This utterance came after a young man asked His help in securing a portion of the possession left behind by his deceased father. Jesus then proceeded to tell the story of the prosperous farmer who amassed wealth that couldn't prevent him from dying. Jesus declared that anyone who amasses riches but is not rich toward God is foolish.

In commenting on the above parable, Ellen White explains, "The desire to obtain money is a snare of Satan, and one that is most popular in these last days. The selfishness which the desire for gain begets, removes the favour of God from the church, and deadens spirituality. To live for self is to perish. Covetousness, the desire for benefit for self's sake, cuts the soul off from life. It is the spirit of Satan to get, to draw to self. It is the spirit of Christ to give, to sacrifice self for the good of others. Wherefore He says, "Take heed, and beware of covetousness; for a man's life consisteth not in the abundance of the things which he possesseth" (AUCR, April 15, 1912).

The Apostle Paul also warns against grasping after money and sets out the dangers of such an attitude. His statements are full of vital instructions for God's people. After warning that those who want to be rich fall into temptation and a snare and into many foolish and hurtful lusts, he admonishes us not to keep company with those who think that "gain is godliness." Next, he tells of those who have left the faith because of their pursuit of money. Then, he asserts that godliness with contentment is great gain. This being the case, we should "follow after righteousness, godliness, faith, love, patience, meekness" and "Fight the good fight of faith..." (1 *Timothy* 6:11-12).

Neither the Bible writers nor Ellen White is saying that it is a sin to make money. However, the wrong attitude, motive, and approach to making money is dangerous. The following paragraph from Mrs. White sums up the correct attitude and use: "It is God who gives men power to get wealth, and He has bestowed this ability, not as a means of gratifying self, but as a means of returning to God His own. With this object it is not a sin to acquire means. Money is to be earned by labour. Every youth should be trained to habits of industry. The Bible condemns no man for being rich if he has acquired his riches honestly. It is the selfish love of money wrongfully employed that is the root of all evil. Wealth will prove a blessing if we regard it as the Lord's, to be received with thankfulness and with thankfulness returned to the Giver.

But of what value is untold wealth if it is hoarded in expensive mansions or in bank stocks? What do these weigh in comparison with the salvation of one soul for whom the Son of the infinite God has died?" (*Testimonies* for the Church 6 453).

Here are some critical insights about money to which all should pay attention:

- Money is essential to our daily lives and is considered by many to be the ultimate goal of life.

- Money possesses elements that may destroy us. It is a problem when used selfishly but is a blessing when used as an agent of service.

- Our attitude to money is an index of our character, and a person will not be entrusted with eternal riches if he or she has not learned to use material resources in harmony with God's directives.

There are two approaches to money that God's people should shun. People preparing for the soon-coming kingdom of God should not spend their money extravagantly or recklessly, whether they have little or much, but especially if they possess great wealth. They should also avoid accumulating unnecessary amounts. Both approaches are dangerous to spiritual life.

As was said earlier, "It is God who gives men power to get wealth, and He has bestowed this ability, not as a means of gratifying self, but as a means or returning to God His own" (Ibid). We should also remember that "Money cannot be carried into the next life; it is not needed there. But the good deeds done in winning souls to Christ are carried to the heavenly courts." Also, "Those who selfishly spend the Lord's gifts on themselves, leaving their fellow creatures without aid and doing nothing to advance God's work in the world, dishonour their maker" *(Christ's Object Lessons*, p. 266).

Ellen White cautioned that "hoarded wealth is not merely useless; it is a curse. In this life it is a curse to the soul, drawing the affections away from the heavenly treasure" (*Ibid*, p. 352). Our Savior admonished us to "...provide yourselves bags which wax not old, a treasure in the heavens that faileth not" (Luke 12:33) and to "Lay not up for yourselves treasures upon earth...But lay up for yourselves treasures in heaven, where neither moth nor rust doth corrupt, and where thieves do not break through nor steal" (Matthew 6:19-20). This advice from Jesus is quite pertinent because "The very means that is now so sparingly invested in the cause of God, and that is selfishly retained, will in a little while be cast with all idols to the moles and to the bats" (Evangelism, p. 63).

Storing up Money and Our Possessions

Both the Bible and Ellen White give very pertinent and valuable advice on how we should store up our money and possessions. Here are a few examples:

Jesus: Luke 12:33

"Sell that ye have, and give alms; provide yourselves bags which wax not old, a treasure in the heavens that faileth not, where no thief approacheth, neither moth corrupteth."

Paul: 1 Timothy 6:17-19

"Charge them that are rich in this world, that they be not highminded, nor trust in uncertain riches, but in the living God, who giveth us richly all things to enjoy; That they do good, that they be rich in good works, ready to distribute, willing to communicate; Laying up in store for themselves a good foundation against the time to come, that they may lay hold on eternal life."

Ellen White:

"Money is a constant test of the affections. Whoever acquires more than sufficient for his real needs should seek wisdom and grace to know his own heart and to keep his heart diligently, lest he have imaginary wants and become an unfaithful steward, using with prodigality his Lord's entrusted capital" *(Adventist Home*, p.372).

"It is now that our brethren should be cutting down their possessions instead of increasing them. We are about to move to a better country, even a heavenly. Then let us not be dwellers upon the earth, but be getting things into as compact a compass as possible. The time is coming when we cannot sell at any price. The decree will soon go forth prohibiting men to buy or sell of any man save he that hath the mark of the beast" *(Testimonies for the Church* 5:152).

Remembering the Source of Our Money

Knowing our tendency to forget the source of our money and possessions and our disposition to be extravagant and wasteful, we must always remember that everything we have comes from the Lord. From the world's creation, the Lord presented to Adam and Eve a special symbol of His ownership of our lives and all we have. It was the "Tree of the Knowledge of Good and Evil" in the midst of the garden. Ellen White explains, "The Lord placed our first parents in the Garden of Eden. He surrounded them with everything that could minister to their happiness, and He bade them acknowledge Him as the possessor of all things. In the garden He caused to grow every tree that was pleasant to the eye or good for food; but among them He made one reserve. Of all else, Adam and Eve might freely eat; but of this one tree God said, "Thou shalt not eat of it." Here was the test of their gratitude and loyalty to God" (*Counsels on Stewardship*, p.65).

This particular tree does not exist anymore, but it is still crucial for people to remember that God is the Creator and Owner, so He has instituted the tithing program. Again, Ellen White explains: "So the Lord has imparted to us heaven's richest treasure in giving us Jesus. With Him He has given us all things richly to enjoy. The productions of the earth, the bountiful harvests, the treasures of gold and silver, are His gifts. Houses and lands, food and clothing, He has placed in the possession of men. He asks us to acknowledge Him as the Giver of all things; and for this reason, He says, of all your possessions I reserve a tenth for Myself, besides gifts and offerings, which are to be brought into My storehouse" (ibid).

We learn the importance of returning the tithe to the Lord in several places in Scripture. A special blessing is promised to those who do, and a dreadful curse is declared upon those who refuse. This blessing is a part of enjoying fullness of life, and the Lord wants us all to have it.

QUESTIONS FOR CONTEMPLATION

1. How important is money?

2. What are some of the dangers associated with chasing riches?

3. What are some of the blessings of possessing wealth?

4. What is the purpose of tithing?

5. Has the tithing programme been a blessing to you?

Chapter 8

Living For the Glory of the Lord

Fullness of life is a gift from God. Jesus said He came so that we might have life and have it more abundantly (John 10:10). Those who enjoy this precious gift will always be inspired to live their lives continually for the glory of God in all places. David boasts, "I will bless the Lord at all times: His praise shall continually be in my mouth" (Psalm 34:1). The apostle Paul presents us with this challenge: "Whether therefore ye eat or drink, or whatsoever ye do, do all to the glory of God" (1 Corinthians 10:31).

We live in the last days of Earth's history, a time of rampant selfishness. According to Apostle Paul, it would be a time when people would be boastful, be consumed by self-love, and be lovers of pleasure instead of being lovers of God (2 Timothy 3:2-

4). This means that there would be much focus on self to the exclusion of God from our lives, a time of great self-exaltation. That is why the first of the "Three Angels Messages" calls upon the world to fear God and give glory to Him (Revelation 14:6).

This matter of giving glory to God has an essential place in the ongoing great controversy between Christ and Satan, which is nearing its end. God is searching for individuals through whom He can display His character, power, and glory to attract sinners to Himself to receive His salvation (2 Chronicles 16:9). Ellen White writes, "Christ has given to the church a sacred charge. Every member should be a channel through which God can communicate to the world the treasures of His grace, the unsearchable riches of Christ…All heaven is waiting for men and women through whom God can reveal the power of Christianity" (*Acts of The Apostles*, 600).

The return of Jesus Christ to end the tragedy of sin is also dependent on God's people living for His glory. This is implied in the following statement from Ellen White: "Were all who profess His name bearing fruit to His glory, how quickly the whole world would be sown with the seed of the gospel. Quickly the last great harvest would be ripened, and Christ would come to gather the precious grain" (*Christ's Object Lessons*, 69).

The great motivation presented to us for living for God's glory is that He is our Creator and Sustainer. Also, the amazing cost of the salvation that He has freely provided for us should constantly inspire us. In Psalms 100:3, we are reminded that "...it is He that has made us and not we ourselves." Paul says that it is in Him that we live and move and have our being (Acts 17:28). Another important motivation is the fact that we are living in the time of God's judgment (Revelation 14:7), a moment when we are each being examined to determine on whose side we are. When we realize the greatness and goodness of God and the cost of our salvation, it is difficult for us to live for self.

With these considerations in mind, we must understand what living for God's glory means. There is much misunderstanding about this in Christianity these days. Some people believe that by singing, clapping, praising, and calling upon God's name, they are living for His glory. Others think that by preaching, attending church, and doing good deeds, they meet the divine criteria for living for His glory. While these are important elements in living for His glory, Jesus utters a warning in the book of Matthew that all should heed: "Not every one that saith unto me, Lord, Lord, shall enter the kingdom of heaven; but he that doeth the will of my Father which is in heaven. Many will say to me in that day, Lord, Lord, have we not prophesied in thy name? and in thy name have cast out devils? and in thy name done many wonderful works? And then will I profess unto them, I never knew you: depart from me, ye that work iniquity"

(Matthew 7:21-23). Therefore, to live for God's glory means more than verbal expressions to Him or about Him.

To properly understand what it means to live for God's glory, we must first understand what constitutes God's glory. Moses had an encounter with God on Mount Sinai that can assist us in this regard. He, Moses, had requested the Lord to show him His glory (Exodus 33:18), and the Lord invited him up to the mountain, where He passed before him in a cloud. Moses made a stunning declaration after His encounter:

"The LORD, The LORD God, merciful and gracious, longsuffering, and abundant in goodness and truth, Keeping mercy for thousands, forgiving iniquity and transgression and sin, and that will by no means clear the guilty; visiting the iniquity of the fathers upon the children, and upon the children's children, unto the third and to the fourth generation."

We learn from this that God's glory is His character, not the dazzling brightness and majesty that surround Him. So, to live for God's glory is to reveal His character in our lives. In response, Ellen White wrote, "There is nothing that the Saviour desires so much as agents who will represent to the world His Spirit and His character. There is nothing that the world needs so much as the manifestation through humanity of the Saviour's love" (*Acts of the Apostles*, 600).

When we live for God's glory, we are Christlike, and "A Christlike life is the most powerful argument that can be advanced in favour of Christianity" (*Testimonies for the Church* 9:21). So, when we live for God's glory, we are showing off for Him, and this attracts others to Jesus. That is why Jesus admonishes us: "Let your light so shine before men that they may see your good works and glorify your Father which is in heaven" (*Matthew* 5:16). One of the results of being Christlike is doing good works. So, again, Ellen White explains: "True worship consists in working together with Christ. Prayers, exhortation, and talk are cheap fruits, which are frequently tied on; but fruits that are manifested in good works, in caring for the needy, the fatherless, and widows, are genuine fruits, and grow naturally upon a good tree" (*Christian Service*, 96).

Still, another aspect of living for God's glory is seeking to please Him in all areas of our lives. It is said that Enoch, before his translation, had this testimony that he pleased God (Hebrews 11:5). This means that in that ungodly age, everyone knew that this man lived to please God. His living to please God inspired others to look to God after God miraculously removed Enoch from society. That is why the apostle Paul directs us, "Whether therefore ye eat or drink, or whatsoever ye do, do all to the glory of God" (1 Corinthians 10:31). With this in mind, we should always be thinking about whether our actions are pleasing to the Lord, or if they bring Him glory, inspiring others to want to serve Him. In all our activities in life, our motivation should not be what we want to do or what pleases us, but what is acceptable to the Lord. Like the twenty-four elders of Revelation, let us remember that God is worthy to receive glory and honour and power: for He has created all things, and for His pleasure we exist and were created (*Revelation* 4:11).

Another critical component of living for God's glory is loving, joyful obedience to His words and loyalty to Him. In Moses' farewell address to the Israelites, he challenged them to carefully obey God's Word so that the surrounding nations were enlightened to see the wisdom of Jehovah, their God, and the superiority of His ways. He declared:

"Behold, I have taught you statutes and judgments, even as the LORD my God commanded me, that ye should do so in the land whither ye go to possess it. Keep therefore and do them; for this is your wisdom and your understanding in the sight of the nations, which shall hear all these statutes, and say, Surely this great nation is a wise and understanding people. For what nation is there so great, who hath God so nigh unto them, as the LORD our God is in all things that we call upon him for? And what nation is there so great, that hath statutes and judgments so righteous as all this law, which I set before you this day?" (*Deuteronomy* 4:5-8).

Moses was saying that Israel's obedience would reveal to the nations the greatness and wisdom of their God and the blessings of obedience. God's people today have the same challenge and privilege. Do people want to serve God and keep His commandments because of how we trust and obey Him and the resulting blessings in our lives?

Another supreme example of someone wanting to serve Jehovah because of how His people related to Him is found in the book of Ruth. Naomi and her husband and sons had migrated to Moab because of a famine in Israel. Sometimes after, her husband and her two sons died, so Naomi decided to return to her homeland. Accordingly, she instructed her daughters-in-law to remain in their native country with their people and their gods. However, Ruth refused, uttering these famous words: "Intreat me not to leave thee, or to return from following after thee: for whither thou goest, I will go; and where thou lodgest, I will lodge: thy people shall be my people, and thy God my God" (Ruth 1:16). Apparently, Ruth's memorable decision and declaration was brought about by Naomi's loyalty to Jehovah and the way she related to Him even facing adverse circumstances in her life.

"The church is God's agency for the proclamation of truth, empowered by Him to do a special work; and if she is loyal to Him, obedient to all His commandments, there will dwell within her the excellency of divine grace. If she will be true to her allegiance, if she will honour the Lord God of Israel, there is no power that can stand against her. (Acts of the Apostles, 600)."

"Those who are watching for the Lord, are purifying their souls by obedience to the truth. With vigilant watching they combine earnest working. Because they know that the Lord is at the door, their zeal is quickened to co-operate with the divine intelligences in working for the salvation of souls." (Chs 95).

So, in concluding this chapter, let us remind ourselves that living for God's glory means that, first and foremost, we acknowledge Him as our Creator, Lord, and Saviour; we joyfully obey Him, showing to the world that His commandments are not grievous and that living for Him brings great blessings to our lives. We seek His guidance in all aspects of our lives, displaying His love to others and revealing that His way is best. This will attract people to make Him the Lord of their lives, and they also will begin living for His glory.

QUESTIONS FOR CONTEMPLATION

1. What does it mean to you to live for God's glory?
2. Is there any aspect of your life that the Lord is not pleased with?
3. Do you consult the Lord before making every important decision?
4. Have you ever regretted any decision you have made?

Chapter 9

Being Extravagant for Jesus

God's amazing love led Him to do the most amazing thing to save us. He gave His only Son to suffer the most ignominious death, eternal death, to bring us everlasting life (*John* 3:16). Also, according to Peter, God, through His divine power "hath given unto us all things that pertain unto life and godliness, through the knowledge of him that hath called us to glory and virtue" (2 Peter 1:3). And Paul asserts that since God did not spare His own Son, but delivered Him up for us all, He will freely give us all things (*Romans* 8:32).

Since God gave us the best, it is more than reasonable that we should do our best for Him, and a person experiencing the fullness of life will endeavor to do and give his best for Jesus. We have several biblical examples of individuals doing their best for

Him. There is the example of the widow who gave all her money to the treasury to support the Lord's work. Her act was so outstanding that it drew the public commendation of Jesus, who praised her as an example for other worshippers.

Probably, the best demonstration in the Bible of someone being extravagant and outstanding for Jesus is the example of Mary Magdalene. Her example is so unique that it is mentioned by all four Gospel writers (*Matthew* 26:6–13, *Mark* 14:3-8, *Luke* 7:36-50, *John* 12:1-8). Mary was a great sinner in the eyes of society. She was a prostitute. Jesus had met her and mercifully delivered her from the demon of prostitution. She was also the sister of Lazarus, whom Jesus had raised from the dead.

In response to these two loving actions of Jesus, Mary publicly showed her deep appreciation to Jesus. She purchased a very expensive bottle of perfume, and when she knew that Jesus was attending a feast at the house of a pharisee, she showed up. Breaking the bottle, she poured out the perfume on His head and feet and used her hair to wipe His feet. So, she was using the most honorable part of her body to wipe the least honorable part of the body of Jesus!

This action of Mary generated much opposition and anger from the host of the feast and some of Jesus' disciples. They thought that because Mary was a great sinner, Jesus should not have allowed her to touch His person. Also, to them, pouring such a costly perfume on Jesus constituted a great waste.

In response to their condemnation of the woman and their criticism of Jesus' acceptance of her appreciation and generosity, He told them that she did what she did because she loved Him much because of what He had done for her. He also told them to leave her alone because she had done her best. On the other hand, Simon, to whom Jesus had shown great mercy in healing him of leprosy, had manifested great ingratitude in how he treated Jesus.

Jesus was so impressed by Mary's action that He predicted that Mary's amazing story would be told wherever the Gospel would be preached. Jesus wanted the story to be told so we would emulate her noble example.

As we contemplate Mary's marvellous demonstration of her love and appreciation, we need to ask ourselves if we are doing our best for Jesus who has so lovingly and mercifully saved us from eternal destruction. In the words of Ellen White, "Greater light shines upon us than shone upon our fathers. We cannot be accepted or honored of God in rendering the same service, or doing the same works, that our fathers did. In order to be accepted and blessed of God as they were, we must imitate their faithfulness and zeal—improve our light as they improved theirs, and do as they would have done had they lived in our day" (*Testimonies 1: 262*).

Here is a challenge from a songwriter of past ages:

I wonder, have I done my best for Jesus,
Who died upon the cruel tree?
To think of His great sacrifice at Calvary!
I know my Lord expects the best from me.
The hours that I have wasted are so many,
The hours I've spent for Christ so few;
Because of all my lack of love for Jesus,
I wonder if His heart is breaking too.
[Refrain]

Ellen White again challenges us, "Let us do while we have the strength. Let us work while it is day. Let us devote our time and our means to the service of God so that we may have His approbation and receive His reward" (*Counsels Stewardship*, p. 21). Another songwriter, Anne Steele (1717-1778), wrote:

My Maker and my King
to Thee my all I owe.
Thy sovereign bounty is the spring;
Whence all my blessings flow;
Thy sovereign bounty is the spring;
Whence all my blessings flow.

The creature of Thy hand,
on Thee alone I live;
My God, Thy benefits demand
more praise than I can give.
My God, Thy benefits demand
more praise than I can give.

Lord, what can I impart
when all is Thine before?
Thy love demands a thankful heart,
the gift, alas! How poor.
Thy love demands a thankful heart,
the gift, alas! How poor.

Oh, let Thy grace inspire
my soul with strength divine;
Let every word each desire
and all my days be Thine.
Let every word each desire
and all my days be Thine.

By God's grace, let us be extravagant for Jesus.

QUESTIONS FOR CONTEMPLATION

1. What is the best thing that Jesus has done for you?

2. What is the best thing you have ever done for Jesus?

3. Have you ever given Jesus a special gift?

4. Do you think it is alright to use your tithe to help the poor?

Chapter 10

Thanksgiving and Living

God has provided many elements to assist us in experiencing the abundant life that Jesus came into the world to give us. Among these is the element of thanksgiving; it is an integral part of the life of every truly converted person. Its absence in the experience of any Christian would suggest that the individual does not acknowledge or recognize the working of God in his or her everyday existence.

It is surprising and alarming to Jesus when we do not offer Him the gratitude that is due to him. This is demonstrated in the story of the healing of the ten lepers recorded in the Gospel of Luke (17:12-18). Jesus met the ten lepers who cried out to Him for mercy since they had become outcasts from society because of this terror that had fallen upon them. Instead of healing them instantly, He requested that they show themselves to the priest. As they went, to their amazement, they were healed, and the one who was a Samaritan turned back to express his gratitude to Jesus. Jesus was so impressed by his action that He uttered these memorable words: "Were there not ten cleansed? But where are the nine? There are not found that returned to give glory to God, save this stranger."

Ellen White's commentary on the story is full of instructions for us: "When the ten lepers came to Jesus for healing, He bade them go and show themselves to the priest. On the way, they were cleansed, but only one returned to give Him glory. The others went their way, forgetting Him who had made them whole." Then she laments, "How many are still doing the same thing!"

According to Ellen White, "If there is anyone who should be continually grateful, it is the follower of Christ," and "If we appreciate or have any sense of how dearly our salvation was purchased, anything which we may call sacrifice will sink away into insignificance" (*Our High Calling, 201*). Furthermore, in another context, she says, "As Jesus views the state of His professed followers today, He sees base ingratitude, hollow formalism, hypocritical insincerity, pharisaical pride and apostasy" (Testimonies for The Church 5:72).

In suggesting that we have many things to be grateful for, she says, "The world is full of dissatisfied spirits who overlook the happiness and blessings within their reach and are continually seeking for happiness and satisfaction that they do not realize...They cherish unbelief and ingratitude in that they overlook the blessings right in their pathway. The common, everyday blessings of life are unwelcome to them, as was the manna to the children of Israel" (2T 640). Therefore, we should be careful to express our gratitude to God for even the small things He provides us daily.

"By their ingratitude, they close their hearts against the grace of God. Like the heath in the desert, they know not when good cometh, and their souls inhabit the parched places of the wilderness (*Desire of Ages, p. 348).*"

Thanksgiving should be a constant part of our daily life, especially when we gather for worship. David says, "Make a joyful noise unto the LORD, all ye lands. Serve the LORD with gladness: come before his presence with singing... Enter into his gates with thanksgiving, and into his courts with praise; be thankful unto him and bless his name. For the LORD is good; his mercy is everlasting..." (Psalm 100:1-5).

David tells us to express our gratitude to the Lord because of His goodness and mercy, which manifest in our lives in many and varied ways. Ellen White reminds us, "The Lord works continually to benefit mankind. He is ever imparting His bounties" (*Desire of Ages*, p. 348).

We should reflect on some of the manifestations of God's blessings in our lives. These include raising us from our sick beds, delivering us from dangers that we do not see, commissioning His heavenly angels to save us from calamity, and guarding us from "the pestilence that walketh in darkness" and "the destruction that wasteth at noonday" (Psalm 91:6). However, if these do not impress our hearts, His greatest blessing should, because "He has given all the riches of heaven to redeem us (*Desire of Ages*, p. 348). If we cannot find anything else to thank God for, we should remember that He has provided eternal life for each of us (*John* 3:16). Without this gift, nothing else matters.

Thanksgiving is so important that the Lord directed the Israelites to assemble three times yearly for special thanksgiving services: "Three times thou shalt keep a feast unto me in the year: Thou shalt keep the feast of unleavened bread: thou shalt eat unleavened bread seven days, as I commanded thee, in the time appointed of the month Abib; for in it thou camest out from Egypt: and none shall appear before me empty; and the feast of harvest, the firstfruits of thy labours, which thou hast sown in the field: and the feast of ingathering, which is in the end of the year, when thou hast gathered in thy labours out of the field" (*Exodus* 23:14-16). These feasts were festivals held annually to remember God's blessings and celebrate His goodness.

According to David, thanksgiving is a good thing. He says: "It is a good thing to give thanks unto the LORD, and to sing praises unto thy name, O most High: To shew forth thy lovingkindness in the morning, and thy faithfulness every night, for thou, LORD, hast made me glad through thy work: I will triumph in the works of thy hands" (Psalm 92:1-2, 4). Also, in Psalm 34, he declares: "I will bless the LORD at all times: his praise shall continually be in my mouth. My soul shall make her boast in the LORD." Then he invites us: "O magnify the LORD with me, and let us exalt his name together" (Psalm 34: 1-3).

So, what is so good about thanksgiving that Jesus and other Bible characters invite us to participate in it? What are the benefits it brings to our lives? It is well for us to remember that while God is pleased by our expression of gratitude, He does not need it! It is for our own good. So, what are some of the benefits that thanksgiving brings to our lives?

In the first place, gratitude enriches our lives. It brings us peace and joy; it relieves us of stress and lightens the burdens of our lives. It even enhances our health. Solomon teaches us that "A merry heart (and thanksgiving makes us merry) doeth good like a medicine" (Proverbs 17:22). Ellen White endorses this notion when she says, "The soul that responds to the grace of God shall be like a watered garden. His health shall spring forth speedily, his light shall rise in obscurity, and the glory of the Lord shall be seen upon him" (*Desire of Ages*, p. 347).

Another blessing of thanksgiving is that it strengthens our faith, enabling us to claim more from God. Because of this, Ellen White says, "It is for our own benefit to keep every gift of God fresh in our memory. Thus, faith is strengthened to claim and to receive more and more. There is greater encouragement for us in the least blessing we ourselves receive from God than in all the accounts we can read of the faith and experience of others" (*Ibid*).

A very important aspect of the life of a Christian is witnessing, and thanksgiving facilitates and enhances our witnessing for Christ. Ellen White says, "Our confession of His faithfulness is Heaven's chosen agency for revealing Christ to the world. We are to acknowledge His grace as made known through the holy men of old; but that which will be most effectual is the testimony of our own experience. We are witnesses for God as we reveal in ourselves the working of a power that is divine" (*Ibid*). She even informs that "God desires that our praise shall ascend to Him, marked by our own individuality. These precious acknowledgments to the praise of the glory of His grace, when supported by a Christ-like life, have an irresistible power that works for the salvation of souls" (*Ibid*).

A significant detail (element) concerning thanksgiving is that it is practical. It is wonderful to speak and sing of the goodness of God, but if we go no further, we fail to give genuine gratitude to the Lord. So, while reviewing his life, David asked himself, "What shall I render unto the Lord for all His benefits toward me?" His answer is very instructive for us, "I will take the cup of salvation and call upon the name of the Lord. I will pay my vows unto the Lord now in the presence of all His people." (Psalms 116:12-14). He is endorsing the point that there is a practical aspect to expressing thanks to God.

Some biblical examples of the practical nature of thanksgiving are evidenced when Hannah returned Samuel to the Lord for as long as he lived, when Mary Magdalene poured on Jesus a very expensive bottle of perfume, and when David himself purchased a lamb to offer His sacrifice to the Lord instead of accepting a free one from a friend. So, we have much to learn from Ellen White's statement when she writes, "The Lord does not need our offerings. We cannot enrich Him by our gifts. Yet God permits us to show our appreciation of His mercies by self-sacrificing efforts to extend the same to others. This is the only way in which it is possible for us to manifest our gratitude and love to God. He has provided no other. *(Counsels on Stewardship*, p. 18).

Fullness of Life

So, as we close this chapter, "Let us then remember the loving-kindness of the Lord and the multitude of His tender mercies. Like the people of Israel, let us set up our stones of witness and inscribe upon them the precious story of what God has wrought for us. And as we review His dealings with us...let us, out of hearts melted with gratitude, declare, what shall I render unto the Lord for all His benefits toward me? I will take the cup of salvation, and call upon the name of the Lord. I will pay my vows unto the Lord now in the presence of all His people." Ps. 116:12-14. (*Desire of Ages*, 348). Let us make thanksgiving a significant part of our lives, so we will take a step closer to experiencing the fullness of life that the Lord wants us to experience.

QUESTIONS FOR CONTEMPLATION

1. Has anyone ever been ungrateful to you?

2. Have you ever been ungrateful to anyone?

3. What are some things you have in your life now that you need to thank God for?

4. Do you feel comfortable talking about what God is doing for you?

Chapter 11

Giving and Living

"Give, and it shall be given unto you; good measure, pressed down, and shaken together, and running over, shall men give into your bosom. For with the same measure that ye mete withal it shall be measured to you again."
(Luke 6:38)

Giving is not natural to the human spirit but essential to living. Trees reproduce themselves by producing fruit for man. These fruits have seeds that grow into new trees. The Dead Sea is so named because it takes in water but does not give out any. Human beings who take in food but do not excrete and sweat will become sick and eventually die.

According to Ellen White, the whole universe operates on the principle of giving. She says, "All things both in heaven and in earth declare that the great law of life is a law of service. The infinite Father ministers to the life of every living thing. Christ came to the earth "as He that serveth." (Luke 22:27). The angels are "...ministering spirits, sent forth to minister for them who shall be heirs of salvation." (Hebrews 1:14). The same law of service is written upon all things in nature. The birds of the air, the beasts of the field, the trees of the forest, the leaves, the grass, and the flowers, the sun in the heavens and the stars of light—all have their ministry. Lake and ocean, river and water spring—each takes to give. As each thing in nature ministers thus to the world's life, it also secures its own" (Education, 103). It is obvious that by service she means giving. When we serve, we give; by giving, we secure our own lives.

Since giving is essential to living, we can appreciate why God Himself set the example for giving. By creating us, He shared life with us. To redeem us, He gave the life of His Son (John 3:16). The Apostle Paul exclaims, "He that spared not his own Son, but delivered him up for us all, how shall he not with him also freely give us all things?" (Romans 8:32). So, to secure both temporal and spiritual life for us, God gave. Since He gave us the best in Jesus, He will give us anything else that is for our good. And all God's gifts will assist us in attaining the fullness of life Christ promised.

Our Response to God's Gifts

As David reviewed his life one day, his heart swelled up with gratitude for God's marvelous mercies and blessings. His natural question was, "What shall I render unto the Lord for all His benefits toward me?" (Psalm 116:12). That is the reasonable question from every grateful heart. Everyone who truly acknowledges God's goodness will want to respond to Him. David's first response was to "take the cup of salvation and call upon the name of the Lord" (Psalm 116:13). That means giving himself to the Lord. Next, he committed to paying his vows to the Lord (verse 14). Ellen White explains: "The Lord does not need our offerings. We cannot enrich Him by our gifts...Yet God permits us to show our appreciation of His mercies by self-sacrificing efforts to extend the same to others. This is the only way in which it is possible for us to manifest our gratitude and love to God" (*Counsels on Stewardship*, 18).

Motivation for Giving

Some people find it difficult to give. This may be because they are naturally selfish or do not think they have enough to give. Whatever their situation, when they develop a certain basic understanding, they will give, even when they have only a little.

Our first motivation for giving is that all we have has been freely given to us by God. The Bible teaches, "...freely ye have received, freely give" (*Matthew* 10:8). David understood this when, after witnessing the generous gifts brought for the building of the temple, he declared to the Lord, "...for all things come of Thee, and of Thine own have we given thee" (1 Chronicles 29:14).

Another important basis for giving is God's great mercies. This is what Paul uses to challenge the brethren in Rome: "I beseech you therefore, brethren, by the mercies of God, that ye present your bodies a living sacrifice, holy, acceptable unto God, which is your reasonable service." (Romans 12:1). It is because of God's mercies that we are alive, so we should be happy to return our lives to Him in living service. We should always remember that it is because God loves us that He gave His Son (John 3:16). His mercy should inspire love and gratitude in our hearts, which will inspire us to give.

If we are not giving, it may be because we are not loving, for all loving results in giving.

The Benefits of Giving

We should not give because we want the benefits of giving. However, giving naturally results in a blessing to the giver. Several Bible passages speak about this:

Jesus admonished His followers, "Give, and it shall be given unto you; good measure, pressed down, and shaken together, and running over, shall men give into your bosom" (Luke 6:38). And the Apostle Paul quotes Jesus as saying, "It is more blessed to give than to receive" (Acts 20:35).

Solomon was very insightful when he wrote, "The liberal soul shall be made fat: and he that watereth shall be watered also himself." (Proverbs 11:25). Ellen White concurs when she wrote, "None need fear that their liberality would bring them to want. Obedience to God's commandments would surely result in prosperity."

Because Jesus wants us to enjoy the benefits of giving, He expects us to give, even when we have to do it sacrificially. God directed the widow of Zarephath to share her last meal with Elijah. She obeyed, and she and her son were signally blessed; they had food throughout a famine that lasted over three years. (1 Kings 17:8-17). Jesus commended another widow who gave her last two mites as offerings in the synagogue one Sabbath (Mark 12:41-44). The following statement by Ellen White carries the same idea of requiring our offerings to bless us: "True liberality in the follower of Christ identifies his interest with that of his Master...The light of the gospel shining from the cross of Christ rebukes selfishness and encourages liberality and benevolence. It is not to be a lamented fact that there are increasing calls to give...Worldliness and covetousness are eating out the vitals of

God's people. They should understand that His mercy multiplies the demands for their means" (3T-405).

The ability to give has been given to us by God to test, bless, and prepare us for His kingdom. Let us embrace the opportunity to give to others and give back to God. Fullness of life includes the material and spiritual blessings that result from giving: "Let us give while we have the power. Let us do this while we have the strength. Let us work while it is day. Let us devote our time and our means to the service of God, that we may have His approbation, and receive His reward...We should never forget that we are placed on trial in this world, to determine our fitness for the future life. None can enter heaven whose characters are defiled by the foul blot of selfishness. Therefore, God tests us here, by committing to us temporal possessions, that our use of these may show whether we can be entrusted with eternal riches" (Counsels on Stewardship, 21).

QUESTIONS FOR CONTEMPLATION

1. How important is giving in the life of the Christian?
2. Why does God expect us to give?
3. Should we give to receive, or should we receive to give?
4. What remarkable examples of giving can you list from the Bible.

5. Do you enjoy giving things to others?

6. Do you enjoy receiving gifts?

Chapter 12

The Joys and Blessings of Obedience

God has always required obedience of His children. From the day He created Adam and Eve, He gave them directives on how to live. Some of the directives were implied, and some were clearly stated. One command that He made plain was the one that specified their diet, which excluded certain items. Another command that was implied related to the way they should worship. Throughout the Bible, we find commandments that direct all aspects of our lives.

God did not give instructions for our lives just to show that He is the boss and has the right to dictate to us. All His commandments are given for our good. They bring joy and gladness to our experience here on earth as we prepare to spend eternity with Him in His soon-coming kingdom. That's why

David could say, "I delight to do thy will, O my God: yea, thy law is within my heart." (Psalm 40:8). Also, in the last book of the Bible, Revelation, the Angel told John, "Blessed are they that do his commandments, that they may have right to the tree of life, and may enter in through the gates into the city" (Revelation 22:14).

Some persons find obedience difficult, but even if God's requirements are challenging and demanding, they are designed for our ultimate benefit. Jesus challenges us to walk in the straight and narrow way, for at the end of it is to be found everlasting life, while at the end of the easy way, there is destruction (Matthew 7: 13-14). John also tells us, "For this is the love of God, that we keep his commandments: and his commandments are not grievous" (1 John 5:3). Let us now look at some of the joys and blessings of obeying the commandments of God.

We begin with David, one that the Bible calls "a man after his (God's) own heart" (1 Samuel 13:14). In the nineteenth Psalm, he lists several benefits: "The law of the LORD is perfect, converting the soul: the testimony of the LORD is sure, making wise the simple. The statutes of the LORD are right, rejoicing the heart: the commandment of the LORD is pure, enlightening the eyes. The fear of the LORD is clean, enduring for ever: the judgments of the LORD are true and righteous altogether. More to be desired are they than gold, yea, than much fine gold: sweeter also than honey and the honeycomb. Moreover, by them is thy servant warned: and in keeping of them there is great reward." (Psalm 19:7-11). From these verses, we discover that obeying God's law transforms us, makes us wise, and causes us to rejoice. We also learn that they warn us and are sweeter than honey, and keeping them brings us great rewards in this world and the eternal.

Another list of benefits is to be found in Psalm 119, "I understand more than the ancients, because I keep thy precepts. Thy word is a lamp unto my feet, and a light unto my path. Thy testimonies are wonderful: therefore, doth my soul keep them. The entrance of thy words giveth light; it giveth understanding unto the simple. I rejoice at thy word, as one that findeth great spoil. I hate and abhor lying, but thy law do I love. Seven times a day do I praise thee because of thy righteous judgments. Great peace have they which love thy law: and nothing shall offend them, (Psalm 119: 100-165).

Jesus Himself enlightens us about the joys and blessings of obedience. In Matthew 7:21, He admonishes that only those who do God's will can expect to enter the kingdom of Heaven. In His discussion with a wealthy young man who desired to know the way to have eternal life, Jesus explained to him, "Why callest thou me good? there is none good but one, that is, God: but if thou wilt enter into life, keep the commandments," (Matthew19:16-21). Seeking further clarification about what Jesus said, the young man inquired which of the Ten Commandments (Matthew 19:28-21). These Ten Commandments were given by God to enhance our living here in this world and to assist us in preparing to live in heaven with Him. We must learn to joyfully obey Him here before He can trust us to live in the peace and harmony of heaven. Remember that one little disobedience caused Adam and Eve to be expelled from the Garden of Eden.

Refusal to obey God's commandments deprives us of peace, which we need as we journey through this troubled world. God mourns the pitiful experience of Israel because of their disobedience when He says, "Thus saith the LORD, thy Redeemer, the Holy One of Israel; I am the LORD thy God which teacheth thee to profit, which leadeth thee by the way that thou shouldest go. O that thou hadst hearkened to my commandments! then had thy peace been as a river, and thy righteousness as the waves of the sea:" (Isaiah 48:17-18).

With such great blessings to be obtained from joyfully keeping God's commandments and with such motivation as the marvelous sacrifice of our Lord Jesus Christ, would anyone choose not to render to God that obedience that springs from a grateful heart? Certainly not! This is a part of the fullness of life that Jesus wants us to enjoy here on earth before He takes us to share heaven with Him.

QUESTIONS FOR CONTEMPLATION

1. Do you believe that God wants us to obey all His commandments?

2. Do you enjoy obeying all God's commandments?

3. Which of God's commandments you find difficult to obey?

4. Do you think that in heaven everyone will obey everything God says?

Chapter 13

Worshipping in Spirit and in Truth

Worshipping the Creator has always been a part of the activities of God's creatures. In several places in Scripture, the Bible describes the adoration of the heavenly host for their master. In the book of Job, we are informed that at the creation, "...the morning stars sang together, and all the sons of God shouted for joy" (Job 38:7). In Revelation, several worshipful scenes in heaven are mentioned (Revelation 4,5, 19). These beings worship God because of His goodness, grace, and glory.

The Bible also describes the worship of God as coming from human beings in appreciation of love and mercy, resulting in the great salvation wrought out for us through Jesus Christ. Human beings automatically worship, and if we don't worship God, we will worship other objects. Worshipping God is a privilege, and it should be our pleasure to do so.

Worshipping God is not something we do only when we gather in the house of God or a place designated for such activity. It is a devotion to God expressed through everything we do, wherever we are, and always. It is giving adoration to Him under all circumstances. It is acknowledging Him as our Creator and Sovereign and living for His glory and honor.

The place where we worship is not the most important element in worship; it is the attitude and spirit in which we offer our worship to God. In speaking to the woman He met at the well, Jesus pointed out that true worshippers worship the Father in spirit and truth because God seeks those who worship Him (John 4:23). So, what is meant by worshipping God in spirit and truth?

The acceptable reason for worshipping God must be clear before we offer our worship to Him. Otherwise, our worship will be in vain. In the fourth and fifth chapters of the book of *Revelation*, we are given two reasons for worshipping God: Firstly, "Thou art worthy, O Lord, to receive glory and honour and power, for thou hast created all things, and for thy pleasure they are and were created" (Revelation 4:11). Secondly, "...Worthy is the Lamb that was slain to receive power, and riches, and wisdom, and strength, and honour, and glory, and blessing." (*Revelation* 5:12). So, we are to worship God and Jesus Christ His Son simply because they are our Creator and our Redeemer. In other words, we are totally dependent upon them for our physical and spiritual existence. This acknowledgment will guarantee that our worship is of the right kind and is acceptable.

To worship God in spirit means, firstly, that we worship with the right attitude and motive. We approach Him with reverence and humility. We recognize His superiority and majesty, respect and honor Him for who He is, and appreciate our nothingness, sinfulness, and unworthiness.

Our motive in worshipping God should not be selfish. While God takes pleasure in blessing His children, we should not worship Him because we want to bribe Him into giving something to us. We should worship Him because He deserves it, though He does not need anything from us. In addressing the Athenians on Mars Hill, Paul pointed out that God, who made the world and everything in it, since He is Lord of heaven and earth, does not dwell in temples made with hands. Nor is He worshipped with men's hands, as though He needed anything since He gives to all life, breath, and all things. (Acts 17:24-25). We need God, but He doesn't need us. We should bear this in mind always.

To worship "in truth" means to worship according to the truth, and the Bible helps us understand what truth is. Jesus declared to His disciples that He was the way, the truth, and the life (John

14:6). Therefore, our worship should ascend to the Father through Jesus and be in harmony with His teachings.

In His last public prayer before His crucifixion, Jesus asked His Father to sanctify His disciples through His truth, after which He declared, "...thy word is truth" (John 17:17). Hundreds of years before Jesus made that declaration, David, the leader of God's people, had asserted, "...thy law is the truth" (Psalm 119:142). So, as we worship, we should strive to worship according to the teachings of God's Word and His law.

When we analyze the various ways people worship these last days, it becomes evident that much worship is not in harmony with what Jesus has outlined. That's why the observation of Jesus in Mark 7:7-8 must be considered, and our worship must be evaluated against that background. He says, "...in vain do they worship me, teaching for doctrines the commandments of men. For laying aside the commandment of God, ye hold the tradition of men..."

True worship comes from the heart and is inspired by supreme love for God and a desire to be in harmony with Him. Hence, Jesus' comment, "...This people honoureth Me with their lips, but their heart is far from me" (Mark 7:6). Let us ask God to lead us into a genuine life of worship so that at last we will have the joy of joining the angels of heaven in everlasting worship in heaven.

QUESTIONS FOR CONTEMPLATION

1. Do you enjoy going to church?

2. Why do you go to church?

3. What aspects of your church life pleases you the most?

4. Apart from going to church, where else does worship take place?

5. Are you worshipping in spirit and in truth?

6. What does it mean to worship in truth?

Chapter 14

Succeeding in Difficult Times

According to the Bible, the last days leading up to the return of Jesus would be a time of instability, uncertainty, confusion, and turbulence. The angel Gabriel told Daniel that it would "...be a time of trouble, such as never was since there was a nation even to that same time" (Daniel 12:1). Jesus predicted that just before His coming, there would be upon the earth distress of nations, with perplexity, the sea and the waves roaring, men's heart failing them for fear, and for looking after those things which are coming upon the earth" (Luke 21:25,26). The present conditions in our world indicate that we have come to that time, and it is getting worse daily.

All areas of life are being affected. Economically, the world is in turmoil. Wealthier nations are exploiting the poorer countries, and debts are mounting in most nations. Money has been rapidly losing value, and there is rampant inflation. The debt burden is increasing in most nations, including the great United States of America. Poverty is escalating at an alarming rate, and famine and starvation are afflicting millions. Socially, there is crime and violence, and terrorism is spreading fear, threatening the security of many nations. Mass shootings have become frequent and frightening in the US, and, of course, wars are raging across the globe with the threat of the use of nuclear weapons. Then, diseases, especially lifestyle diseases, are increasing, putting tremendous strain on national budgets and healthcare workers.

One of the big questions confronting individuals and nations is how to achieve stability and security. What can we do to adequately cope with these challenges that threaten our very existence? Can we succeed and excel physically, mentally, materially, and spiritually in these unprecedented, difficult times?

From the day God created this world, He has been making provision for the total wellbeing of His people. Also, He has always been showing up in crises to come to the aid of His people. Sometimes, He works miracles, and at other times, He gives instructions on how to cope successfully. The Garden of Eden was lavishly supplied with abundant, wholesome food and a perfect environment conducive to a totally satisfying life. After the worldwide flood destroyed vegetation, God instructed Noah on providing adequate food. Manna fell from heaven for forty years as the Israelites wandered in the wilderness. Ravens fed Elijah the prophet and was later blessed by God's miraculous intervention to supply food for the widow of Zarephath and her son.

God has always shown up for His people in times of hardship, and He has promised to do so in these final difficult days before the return of Jesus. He declares, "Thus saith the LORD, thy Redeemer, the Holy One of Israel; I am the LORD thy God which teacheth thee to profit, which leadeth thee by the way that thou shouldest go. (Isaiah 48:17) In his prediction of "the time of trouble such as never was," Gabriel also said, "...and at that time thy people shall be delivered, everyone that is found written in the book." (Daniel 12:1). However, there are certain steps that we need to take for us to access the needed help from the Lord.

Firstly, the Apostle Paul challenges us not to be anxious but to present our requests to God with a spirit of thanksgiving. His message is, "Be careful for nothing; but in everything, by prayer and supplication, with thanksgiving let your requests be made known unto God. And the peace of God, which passeth all understanding, shall keep your hearts and minds through Christ Jesus" (Philippians 4:6,7). When the peace of God is keeping our hearts and minds, we will not experience stress and anxiety.

Another principle by which we should live to succeed in difficult times is giving God and His business first place in our lives. Not even our wellbeing should be placed before God's. Jesus is very definite on this. He says, "Therefore, take no thought, saying, What shall we eat? or, What shall we drink? or, Wherewithal shall we be clothed?... But seek ye first the kingdom of God, and his righteousness; and all these things shall be added unto you." (Matthew 6:31-33). When we have the faith to place God and His program first, He obligates Himself to care for our interests.

Next, we need to request His intervention. He challenges us to call upon Him in the day of trouble so He can deliver us. Then we will glorify Him (Psalm 50:15). However, we will only sincerely call for His help if we have a trusting relationship. Those who trust in the Lord will be blessed, and their wants will be supplied (Psalm 34:8). Therefore, trusting in the Lord and not following our own inclination is essential for receiving God's assistance in dealing with the challenges in our experiences. Solomon's advice is very pertinent in this regard: "Trust in the lord with all thine heart; and lean not unto thine own understanding. In all thy ways acknowledge him, and he shall direct thy paths." (Proverbs 3:5-10).

Another vital step in receiving God's help in a crisis is obedience, and if we really trust the Lord, we will obey Him, even though His directives might not seem logical! The story of Gideon illustrates this very clearly. The Midianites were oppressing Israel to the point where the people had to be hiding their food. The angel of the Lord instructed Gideon to go and deliver Israel with an army of only three hundred soldiers! When he did, the result was a marvelous victory for the people of God (Judges 6). This story also reminds us that trials and difficulties in our lives do not indicate that the Lord is not with us.

One aspect of obedience we often overlook is the payment of vows we make to the Lord. So, the Lord also admonishes, "Offer unto God thanksgiving; and pay thy vows unto the most High: And call upon me in the day of trouble: I will deliver thee, and thou shalt glorify me." (Psalms 50:14,15). Closely related to this is the return of our tithes and offerings. Again, the Lord, through His messenger, Ellen White, reminds us:

"There is another matter too often neglected by those who seek the Lord in prayer. Have you been honest with God? By the prophet Malachi the Lord declares, 'Even from the days of your fathers ye are gone away from Mine ordinances, and have not kept them. Return unto Me, and I will return unto you,' saith the Lord of hosts. But if we withhold from Him that which is His own, how can we claim His blessing? If we are unfaithful stewards of earthly things, how can we expect Him to entrust us with the things of heaven? It may be that here is the secret of unanswered prayer." (*Christ's Object Lessons*, p.144).

Therefore, if we expect the Lord to come to our defense at any time, especially in times of difficulties, we should heed the admonition that He gives through the prophet Malachi: "Bring ye all the tithes into the storehouse, that there may be meat in mine house, and prove me now herewith, saith the LORD of hosts, if I will not open you the windows of heaven, and pour you out a blessing, that there shall not be room enough to receive it. And I will rebuke the devourer for your sakes, and he shall not destroy the fruits of your ground; neither shall your vine cast her fruit before the time in the field, saith the LORD of hosts." (Malachi 3:10-11).

The psalmist declares, "For the Lord God is a sun and shield: no good thing will He (God) withhold from them that walk uprightly." (Psalm 84:11). This assures us that God will guide and protect His people through dark and dangerous situations. And David reminds us that "The LORD knoweth the days of the upright: and their inheritance shall be for ever. They shall not be ashamed in the evil time: and in the days of famine, they shall be satisfied." (Psalms 37:18,19).

While fullness of life does not mean that God's people will be supplied with great wealth and have trouble-free lives, Jesus has promised to supply all our needs according to His riches in glory. He wants us to experience stable, stress-free lives. Paul asserts, "But my God shall supply all your need according to his riches in glory by Christ Jesus" (Philippians *4:19*). Peter encourages us to cast "all your care upon him; for he careth for you." (*1 Peter 5:7*).

QUESTIONS FOR CONTEMPLATION

1. Would you consider your whole life to be a success right now?

2. What are some of the difficulties you are experiencing?

3. Do you usually pray about your problems?

4. Are you seriously preparing for the "Time of Trouble" of Daniel 12?

5. Do you think we are in that "Time of Trouble" yet?

6. Has God ever helped you to solve a problem?

Chapter 15

God's Prosperity Program

In the Bible, several references are made about the prosperity of God's children, and David, the greatest king of Israel, prays for the prosperity of God's children in many of the Psalms he wrote. For example, he says, "That our garners may be full, affording all manner of store: that our sheep may bring forth thousands and ten thousands in our streets: That our oxen may be strong to labour; that there be no breaking in, nor going out; that there be no complaining in our streets." (Psalm 144:13-14). The Apostle John expresses his desire for one of God's daughters that, above all things, she should prosper and be healthy, even as her soul prospers (3 John 22).

The above references and other Scriptures clearly show that part of God's plan for His people is that they should experience material prosperity while living here on earth. Material satisfaction is an integral component of the abundant life that

Christ has promised to His people. However, spiritual prosperity always takes precedence over material prosperity.

Before we examine what constitutes this prosperity program God desires for His children, we need to understand what material prosperity means to God. As in other aspects of God's plan for His children, there is much misunderstanding about what is involved in prosperity. Many preachers of the Gospel, especially those who operate mega-churches and perform like movie stars on television, preach what is referred to as the "prosperity gospel." To them, the evidence of a successful Christian life is great material wealth, and they focus on it to the exclusion of other essential elements in serving the Lord. However, a careful analysis of Scripture does not support this approach.

A careful examination of Scripture shows that most of God's people were not excessively rich, and many of the faithful mentioned in the Bible were poor and humble. Individuals like Hannah and Elkanah (the parents of Samuel), the parents of Jesus Christ, the widow of Zarephath, the twelve apostles, and the widow who gave her two mites never possessed great wealth. However, they were regarded as faithful servants of God. So, we should be careful not to highlight great wealth as an indication of a very successful Christian life. Also, Jesus reminds us that it is hard for a rich man to be saved (Mark 10: 25) and that one's life does not consist of the material things that he or she possesses (Luke 12:15). Why would Jesus have made these statements if He thought that great wealth was an essential component of Christian experience?

Solomon, probably the wealthiest man who ever lived, requested of the Lord, "…give me neither poverty nor riches; feed me with food convenient for me: Lest I be full, and deny thee, and say, Who is the LORD? or lest I be poor, and steal, and take the name of my God in vain." (Proverbs 30:8-9). From this, we may conclude that, as someone has said, "Prosperity is having what we need when we need it," and sometimes, God gives us more than that.

Despite the preceding, Scripture indicates that God wants His people to be materially satisfied. In his farewell address to Israel, Moses declared, "And the LORD thy God will make thee plenteous in every work of thine hand, in the fruit of thy body, and in the fruit of thy cattle, and in the fruit of thy land…" (Deuteronomy 30:9). It is evident from the passage that it is God who makes His people truly prosperous. Again, Moses is clear: "But thou shalt remember the LORD thy God: for it is he that giveth thee power to get wealth…" (Deuteronomy 8:18). David reinforces the same notion when he says, "Happy is that people, that is in such a case: yea, happy is that people, whose God is the LORD." (Psalms 144:15). The Gospel prophet Isaiah agrees when he states, "Thus saith the LORD, thy Redeemer, the Holy One of Israel; I am the LORD thy God which teacheth thee to profit, which leadeth thee by the way that thou shouldest go." (Isaiah 48:17).

So what is God's prosperity program? It is simple and straightforward, as with all of God's other initiatives. Moses did not only tell Israelites that Jehovah would prosper them. He also outlined to them that it was dependent on their obedience to His words: "Keep therefore the words of this covenant, and do them, that ye may prosper in all that ye do." (Deuteronomy 29:9). This means that we must be careful to carry out His commands, and one of God's commandments that is critically linked to our material prosperity is the command to return our tithes and offerings. In Malachi, the last book of the Old Testament, the Lord confronts His people: "Bring ye all the tithes into the storehouse, that there may be meat in mine house, and prove me now herewith, saith the LORD of hosts, if I will not open you the windows of heaven, and pour you out a blessing, that there shall not be room enough to receive it. And I will rebuke the devourer for your sakes, and he shall not destroy the fruits of your ground; neither shall your vine cast her fruit before the time in the field, saith the LORD of hosts. And all nations shall call you blessed: for ye shall be a delightsome land, saith the LORD of hosts" (Malachi 3:10-12).

Solomon embraces the same principle, as he writes, "Honour the LORD with thy substance, and with the firstfruits of all thine increase: So shall thy barns be filled with plenty, and thy presses shall burst out with new wine." (Proverbs 3:9-10). So, God requires us to use a portion of what He gives to provide financial support for his work. When we do this, it will result in further blessings and will not make us worse.

Being kind and generous to others is another basis on which God's promised fullness of life is experienced. Solomon taught this principle to the people of Israel when he stated, "There is that scattereth, and yet increaseth; and there is that withholdeth more than is meet, but it tendeth to poverty. The liberal soul shall be made fat: and he that watereth shall be watered also himself." (Proverbs 11:24-25). Jesus endorses it by declaring, "Give, and it shall be given unto you; good measure, pressed down, and shaken together, and running over, shall men give into your bosom..." (Luke 6:38). That's why the Apostle Paul could quote Jesus as saying, "It is more blessed to give than to receive" (Acts 20:35). He made this reference after pointing out to them that as working people, they ought to be supporting the brethren who were financially weak.

Some people may think that sharing their material resources with others will make them poorer. However, the opposite is true. Ellen White underscores this point when she writes, "None need fear that their liberality would bring them to want. Obedience to God's commandments (to assist the poor) would surely result in prosperity" (PP 533).

While we should not make the accumulation of wealth our passion, there is nothing wrong with seeking to have adequate financial resources. However, our motive to increase our resources should not be primarily selfish. Uppermost in our minds should be the ability to support God's work and assist the needy. We are blessed to be a blessing, and when we put the interest of God and others before our own, Jesus says that other things will be added to us to care for ourselves and our families. Also, this will assist us in securing everlasting prosperity.

QUESTIONS FOR CONTEMPLATION

1. How do you explain biblical prosperity?
2. Are you a prosperous person?
3. What section of God's prosperity program you find most difficult?
4. Have you ever been blessed by giving away anything?
5. Do you believe that the tithing program really blesses people?

Chapter 16

Laying up Treasures in Heaven

One essential aspect of enjoying the abundant life that Jesus promised His followers is having treasures laid up in heaven. This is important because this earth is destined for destruction, and only those who have treasures laid up in heaven will survive the destruction on earth and make it to heaven. Malachi and Peter make it clear that this planet and everything here will be destroyed (Malachi 4:1-3, 2 Peter 3:10-13). So, it is in our interest to discover what it means to lay up treasures in heaven and how to go about doing so.

How, therefore, can we lay up treasures in heaven? Let us begin our search by hearing from Jesus, our Saviour, who has our best interest at heart. His admonition is: "Sell that ye have and give alms; provide yourselves bags which wax not old, a treasure in the heavens that faileth not, where no thief approacheth, neither moth corrupteth. For where your treasure is, there will your heart be also. In responding to the **rich** young ruler who inquired about what he should do to secure eternal life, Jesus said unto him, "If thou wilt be perfect, go and sell that thou hast, and give to the poor, and thou shalt have treasure in heaven: and come and follow me" (Matthew 19:21).

The Apostle supported this approach when he wrote to Timothy, instructing him to "Charge them that are rich in this world, that they be not highminded, nor trust in uncertain riches, but in the living God, who giveth us richly all things to enjoy; That they do good, that they be rich in good works, ready to distribute, willing to communicate; Laying up in store for themselves a good foundation against the time to come, that they may lay hold on eternal life. (1 Timothy 6:17-19).

Another way to lay up treasures in heaven is as Ellen White explains: "Money cannot be carried into the next life; it is not needed there; but the good deeds done in winning souls to Christ are carried to the heavenly courts." She further explains, "The work of God is to become more extensive, and if His people follow His counsel, there will not be much means in their possession to be consumed in the final conflagration. All will have laid up their treasure where moth and rust cannot corrupt; and the heart will not have a cord to bind it to earth." (Counsels on Stewardship, p. 60). This confirms that using our money to support evangelistic activities is one way of laying up treasures in heaven.

If we remain faithful to the Lord down through the final crisis, we will not be able to utilize our money and material resources then, and we will not be able to contribute them to the cause of God at that time. Therefore, it is wise for us to do so now. Ellen White, in harmony with Bible prophecies, informs us that:

"Houses and lands will be of no use to the saints in the time of trouble, for they will then have to flee before infuriated mobs, and at that time their possessions cannot be disposed of to advance the cause of present truth" She further states that she "…was shown that it is the will of God that the saints should cut loose from every encumbrance before the time of trouble comes, and make a covenant with God through sacrifice. If they have their property on the altar, and earnestly inquire of God for duty, He will teach them when to dispose of these things. Then they will be free in the time of trouble and have no clogs to weigh them down." (CS 59.4).

In this context, Jesus challenges us to learn valuable lessons from the reaction of Lot's wife when she refused to heed God's instruction to flee from Sodom. Those unwilling to lay up treasures in heaven in these last days in a little while will regret that decision. This other warning from Ellen White should be taken very seriously. She states: "I saw that if any held on to their property, and did not inquire of the Lord as to their duty, He would not make duty known, and they would be permitted to keep their property, and in the time of trouble it would come up before them like a mountain to crush them, and they would try to dispose of it, but would not be able. I heard some mourn like this: "The cause was languishing, God's people were starving for the truth, and we made no effort to supply the lack; now our property is useless. O that we had let it go and laid up treasure in heaven!" (CS 60.1)

We do ourselves well to remember that our adversary, the devil, is always seeking to prevent us from embracing the programs that God has set out for our material and spiritual well-being. Here is his strategy: "Go, make the possessors of lands and money drunk with the cares of this life. Present the world before them in its most attractive light, that they may lay up their treasure here, and fix their affections upon earthly things. We must do our utmost to prevent those who labour in God's cause from obtaining means to use against us." (*Counsels on Stewardship*, 154). We must ask the Lord for faith to deny ourselves and resist the devil.

Another approach that contributes to laying up treasures in heaven is using our talents and abilities to serve the Lord. Again, Ellen White is very appropriate. She reminds that Jesus "Taught all to look upon themselves as endowed with precious talents, which, if rightly employed would secure for them eternal riches. He weeded all vanity from life, and by His own example taught that every moment of time is fraught with eternal results; that it is to be cherished as a treasure, and to be employed for holy purposes." *(Christian Service, 120)*. She asked us to remember that "in making a profession of faith in Christ, we pledge ourselves to become all that it is possible for us to be as workers for the Master, and we should cultivate every faculty to the highest degree of perfection, that we may do the greatest amount of good of which we are capable. The Lord has a great work to be done, and He will bequeath the most in the future life to those who do the most faithful, willing service in the present life.) *COL 329)*.

God's directive to His people to use their financial resources in a way that will result in their laying up treasures in heaven is in keeping with the example that the Lord Jesus Himself has set. Paul describes it very well in his letter to the Corinthian brethren: "For ye know the grace of our Lord Jesus Christ, that, though he was rich, yet for your sakes he became poor, that ye through his poverty might be rich." (2 Corinthians 8:9). Jesus gave up eternal riches to live the life of the poorest on earth. This was done to secure eternal riches for us. In turn, He asks us not to allow the riches of the world, which will soon be destroyed, to prevent us from receiving eternal riches. Let us be wise unto salvation.

QUESTIONS FOR CONTEMPLATION

1. Do you think that we will need money in heaven? Why or why not?

2. What are you doing to lay up treasures in heaven?

3. How much of your treasure is on earth, and how much is up in heaven?

4. Do you think that when we tithe, we are laying up treasures in heaven?

5. How good are you at making money?

6. What are some of the dangers associated with having a great wealth?

Chapter 17

Facing the End Time Financial Challenges

Both the Bible and the writings of Ellen White make it clear that money and material things will be sources of great challenges for God's people in the last days. Deteriorating economic conditions, greed, and covetousness will engulf the world, and unfortunately, some of God's people will be negatively impacted. This being the case, our main concern should be how to prepare to survive the onslaught that Satan will make on the people of God through these mediums.

In the coming financial crisis predicted by John in Revelation 13 and other Bible prophets, the rich and the poor, Christians and non-Christians, will come under tremendous pressure as they seek to respond to the challenges. Our attitude to money now and our approach will determine whether the Lord intervenes to assist us.

By God's grace, we must develop the right attitude and craft the correct approach to using the possessions we have been given by God. A wrong attitude and approach will lead to misuse of these resources, which have been lent to us by our Creator for a limited time. We must also appreciate that how we use these possessions will determine our eternal destiny. A correct attitude and use will result in our spending an eternity with Jesus, while an improper use will result in eternal destruction.

To help His disciples develop the right attitude toward material things, Jesus cautioned them that heaven and earth would pass away, but His words would not (Luke 21:33). If material things are going to be destroyed, we cannot keep them forever, even if we live forever. He further warned them not to allow their hearts to be overcharged with the cares of this life; otherwise, the day of His coming would catch them off guard.

According to Ellen White, "Money will soon depreciate very suddenly when the reality of eternal scenes opens to the senses of man" (*Evangelism, p. 63)*. Therefore, it is not wise to spend our time building up massive financial and material resources in these closing days of earth's history. The Prophet of Patmos, John, informs us of a time when the two beasts, mentioned in chapter thirteen of his book, will cause "...all, both small and great, rich and poor, free and bond, to receive a mark in their right hand, or in their foreheads: And that no man might buy or sell, save he that had the mark, or the name of the beast, or the number of his name. (Revelation 13:16-17). This will result in extreme hardship for God's faithful remnant because they will not be able to engage in economic activities. The prophet also informs us that the day is coming when man shall cast his idols of silver and his idols of gold to the moles and the bats (Isaiah 2:20). So, the ungodly will not benefit from the money that they will deprive God's people of using.

Given this coming final crisis when God's faithful, commandment-keeping people will be deprived of using their money, and material things will be useless to everyone, Jesus encourages us to "sell that ye have and give alms; provide yourselves bags which wax not old, a treasure in the heavens that faileth not, where no thief approacheth, neither moth corrupteth. For where your treasure is, there will your heart be also." (Luke 12:33-34).

In looking ahead to that time, Ellen White tells us that "The work of God is to become more extensive, and if His people follow His counsel, there will not be much means in their possession to be consumed in the final conflagration. All will have laid up their treasure where moth and rust cannot corrupt; and the heart will not have a cord to bind it to earth." (1T 197).

This means that if we use our excess resources to finance the expanding work of God before we are deprived of it, there will not be much left to be destroyed in the destruction that will occur at the return of Jesus.

At no time in the history of this world should God's people make material things their priority. And especially now, our main concern should be preparing for the soon return of Jesus while using our money to build up His kingdom. That's why Jesus says to us, "...Take no thought for your life, what ye shall eat, or what ye shall drink; nor yet for your body, what ye shall put on. Is not the life more than meat, and the body than raiment?" (Matthew 6:25)

This counsel from Ellen White should receive our careful attention:

"The desire to obtain money is a snare of Satan, and one that is most popular in these last days. The selfishness which the desire for gain begets, removes the favour of God from the church, and deadens spirituality. To live for self is to perish. Covetousness, the desire for benefit for self's sake, cuts the soul off from life. It is the spirit of Satan to get, to draw to self. It is the spirit of Christ to give. Therefore, He says, 'Take heed, and beware of covetousness; for a man's life consisteth not in the abundance of the things which he possesseth'" (*AUCR, April 15, 1912*)

There is danger in making money-making our priority, especially in these last days. Again, this counsel from Ellen White is very insightful and helpful: "It is this increasing devotion to money getting, the selfishness which the desire for gain begets, that deadens the spirituality of the church, and removes the favor of God from her. When the head and hands are constantly occupied with planning and toiling for the accumulation of riches, the claims of God and humanity are forgotten" (*Counsels on Stewardship*, 20.3).

The signs of the times indicate that we have come to the beginning of this predicted end-time financial crisis. So how should we approach life, and what should be our attitude and approach to money and material things at this time? The best way to prepare for the end time financial crisis is to live as persons waiting for their Lord to come. How would we live if we knew Jesus was going to come tomorrow, next week, or next year? God's words in the Bible and Ellen White's writings are very enlightening and helpful.

Jesus admonishes, "Seek ye first the kingdom of God and His righteousness, and all these things shall be added unto you" (*Matthew* 6:33). If we prioritize God's business in our lives, God will take care of us. Any sacrifice to support His work will be more than adequately rewarded.

Paul instructed Timothy to "Charge them that are rich in this world, that they be not high-minded, nor trust in uncertain riches, but in the living God, who giveth us richly all things to enjoy; That they do good, that they be rich in good works, ready to distribute, willing to communicate; Laying up in store for themselves a good foundation against the time to come, that they may lay hold on eternal life." (1 Timothy 6:17-19). When we use our resources to assist less fortunate people, we secure our future and lay hold on eternal life.

Ellen White again advises, "We ought now to be heeding the injunction of our Saviour: 'Sell that ye have and give alms; provide yourselves bags which wax not old, a treasure in the heavens that faileth not.' It is now that our brethren should be cutting down their possessions instead of increasing them.

Hoarded wealth will soon be worthless. When the decree shall go forth that none shall buy or sell except they have the mark of the beast, very much means will be of no avail. God calls for us now to do all in our power to send forth the warning to the world." *(Last Day Events, 148.)*

"Houses and lands will be of no use to the saints in the time of trouble, for they will then have to flee before infuriated mobs, and at that time their possessions cannot be disposed of to advance the cause of present truth."

"I was shown that it is the will of God that the saints should cut loose from every encumbrance before the time of trouble comes and make a covenant with God through sacrifice. If they have their property on the altar, and earnestly inquire of God for duty, He will teach them when to dispose of these things. Then they will be free in the time of trouble and have no clogs to weigh them down." (CS 59.4)

"We are about to move to a better country, even a heavenly. Then let us not be dwellers upon the earth, but be getting things into as compact a compass as possible. The time is coming when we cannot sell at any price. The decree will soon go forth prohibiting men to buy or sell of any man save him that hath the mark of the beast" (5T 152.2)

Finally, Jesus advises: "Remember Lot's wife. Whosoever shall seek to save his life shall lose it; and whosoever shall lose his life shall preserve it." *(Luke 17:32-33)*. If we think we can secure our lives by selfishly clinging to our resources in opposition to the Word of God, we are deceiving ourselves. Let us trust God and heed His counsel. God commanded Lot and His family to escape from Sodom, leaving behind everything they had worked for, because He was going to destroy the city. Mrs. Lot thought God was asking too much, and she could not afford it. She was reluctant; hence, she perished in the flames. If we are too tied to our money and possessions, we will end up like her, losing heaven and earth. Let us be wise and heed the warning.

QUESTIONS FOR CONTEMPLATION

1. What are some of the financial problems that God's end time people will face?

2. How are you preparing for that time?

3. How much money do you think you will need to survive at that time?

4. What lessons can we learn from Mrs. Lot about end time relationship to money and material things?

Chapter 18

Rejoicing in Tribulation

A comprehensive survey of Bible teachings on the subject of trials and tribulations reveals that God has beneficial purposes in allowing trials to come upon His children. They are not intended to destroy us but to bring us closer to Jesus. What they do to us depends on what we are made of spiritually and our attitude to them. As some observers of human behaviors say, "The same sun that melts the butter hardens the clay." Like the sun, the trials are not the problem; it is the nature of the clay or the butter because of what each is made of! So, we shouldn't blame the trials. So let us now examine what the Bible teaches on the purpose and benefits of trials.

Let's begin with what Jesus, our Saviour, teaches in this regard. Matthew records Jesus as saying in His sermon on the Mount, "Blessed are ye, when men shall revile you, and persecute you, and shall say all manner of evil against you falsely, for my sake.

Rejoice, and be exceeding glad: for great is your reward in heaven: for so persecuted they the prophets which were before you." (Matthew 5:11-12). Three benefits are highlighted here. Firstly, trials bring blessings to our lives; secondly, if we endure, we will have a great reward in heaven; and thirdly, trials elevate us into the exalted company of the Old Testament prophets.

Paul describes many benefits of trials. In Romans, chapter 5, he outlines, "...we glory in tribulations also: knowing that tribulation worketh patience; And patience, experience; and experience, hope;" (Romans 5:3-4). He is saying that trials help us learn to wait on the Lord and fortify our hope in Him. It also enriches our Christian experience. Considering these benefits of tribulations, we can better appreciate how Paul and Silas could be singing in the night in the jail at Philippi after they were severely beaten and thrown into that horrible place, not having committed any crime except preaching the good news about Jesus. To demonstrate their appreciation of the suffering they were encountering, they sang songs of praise to God in the prison. They had every reason to moan and complain, but they didn't!

Again, Apostle Paul, who endured many trials throughout his life, helps us understand the proper response to the trials that we will face as followers of Christ. He states, "...we glory in tribulations also: knowing that tribulation worketh patience" (Romans 5:3).

So, how do we develop this attitude of rejoicing when called upon to endure trials for Christ's sake? First, we must learn about the purpose and benefits of trials.

The apostle Peter, who himself, according to tradition, was by his request crucified upside down, advises believers everywhere to "…rejoice, inasmuch as ye are partakers of Christ's sufferings; that, when his glory shall be revealed, ye may be glad also with exceeding joy. If ye be reproached for the name of Christ, happy are ye; for the spirit of glory and of God resteth upon you: on their part he is evil spoken of, but on your part, he is glorified" (1 Peter 4:13-14). However, he cautions, "But let none of you suffer as a murderer, or as a thief, or as an evildoer, or as a busybody in other men's matters. Yet if any man suffers as a Christian, let him not be ashamed; but let him glorify God on this behalf" (1 Peter 4:15-16).

Job, that Old Testament patriarch who was especially targeted by the devil and whom the Lord permitted to suffer the cruelest onslaught of Satan, apparently understood that there are blessings to be obtained from trials when we do not bring them on ourselves. In the height of his suffering, he was able to say, "But he knoweth the way that I take: when he hath tried me, I shall come forth as gold." (Job 23:10). He was saying that his trials would result in his purification, as when gold is put through the fire for the dross in it to be consumed.

Ellen White writes much about the benefits of trials to God's people, especially those who would be living just before the return of Jesus. Among the benefits, she lists: "God's love for His church is infinite. His care over His heritage is unceasing. He suffers no affliction to come upon the church but such as is essential for her purification, her present and eternal good. He will purify His church even as He purified the temple at the beginning and close of His ministry on earth. All that He brings upon the church in test and trial comes that His people may gain deeper piety and more strength to carry the triumphs of the cross to all parts of the world." (Testimonies for the Church 9:228 (1909)). In addition, she explains that "Afflictions, crosses, temptations, adversity, and our varied trials are God's workmen to refine us, sanctify us, and fit us for the heavenly garner." (Last Day Events, 153, 154).

Speaking of the final onslaught of the Dragon on the final generation of the people of God, she postulates that, "The assaults of Satan are fierce and determined, his delusions are terrible; but the Lord's eye is upon his people, and his ear listens to their cries. Their affliction is great, the flames of the furnace seem about to consume them; but the Refiner will bring them forth as gold tried in the fire. God's love for his children during the period of their severest trial is as strong and tender as in the days of their sunniest prosperity; but it is needful for them to be placed in the furnace fire; their earthliness must be consumed that the image of Christ may be perfectly reflected." (Great Controversy, 621).

If trials benefit God's people, we should not groan and complain; we should be thankful for them, knowing that if we suffer with Christ, we shall also reign with Him. While we should not seek out trials, we should welcome them when they come, asking God for grace to endure them so that they may have a beneficial impact on our lives. Let us, like Paul and Silas, learn to sing in the night.

QUESTIONS FOR CONTEMPLATION

1. What are some of the benefits of trials?

2. Give a reason why God will allow the final generation of Christians to pass through such severe trials?

3. Why does God allow some of His people to be killed, but delivers others like Daniel?

4. Have you ever been brought into difficulties because of your faith?

5. When are trials not beneficial to us?

6. How does a wrong attitude to trials affect their impact on us?

Chapter 19

Aids For Attaining Fullness of Life

God has always desired the best for His people and has always provided for our highest physical, mental, and spiritual development. The apostle Peter assures us that God has given us everything pertaining to life and godliness (2 Peter 1:3).

When the Lord raised up His remnant church, He introduced several programs to assist His people in becoming the special people He had called them to be. These programs include Health Reform, Systematic Benevolence, Christian Education, and Evangelism. Let's look at these programs, beginning with the healthful living program.

David declared, "Bless the Lord, O my soul, and forget not all his benefits: Who forgiveth all thine iniquities; who healeth all thy diseases; Who redeemeth thy life from destruction; who crowneth thee with lovingkindness and tender mercies; Who satisfieth thy mouth with good things; so that thy youth is renewed like the eagle's." (Psalms 103:2-5). Here, we see that God is interested in our health and well-being.

Ellen White wrote over a hundred years ago: "Health is a treasure. Of all temporal possessions, it is the most precious. Wealth, learning, and honor are dearly purchased at the loss of the vigor of health. None of these can secure happiness, if health is lacking." (Counsels on Diet and Foods, p. 20). After our salvation, our health is the most important thing we possess, and no one can experience fullness of life if health is lacking. Despite that, millions continue to sacrifice their health to acquire other temporal possessions.

Health is the foundation of life; with it, we are prepared to accomplish all the other worthwhile goals of life. Without it, we will never achieve our full potential; education, money, and all other attainments will not be thoroughly enjoyed and may be useless. We all see rich and well-educated people who are not enjoying their wealth or education because of ill health. That's why the Lord, in His wisdom and mercy, gave a special health program to His people.

This program was not given merely to secure physical health but to facilitate the total development of our lives—physically, mentally, emotionally, and spiritually. As Ellen White explains, "Let it ever be kept before the mind that the great object of hygienic reform is to secure the highest possible development of mind and soul and body. All the laws of nature—which are the laws of God—are designed for our good. Obedience to them will promote our happiness in this life, and will aid us in a preparation for the life to come." (Christian Temperance and Bible Hygiene, 120).

God wants His people to be healthy. We were created to be healthy, but sickness has come as a result of sin. The apostle John wishes, above all things, that believers may prosper and be in health, even as their souls prosper (3 John 2). The psalmist says that God forgives our iniquities and heals our diseases (Psalms 103:3). Before healing the paralytic that was brought to Him for healing, Jesus forgave him of his sins. All three episodes link physical and spiritual health, suggesting that one cannot exist without the other. And again, in this connection, Ellen White is clear: "He who cherishes the light which God has given him upon health reform has an important aid in the work of becoming sanctified through the truth, and fitted for immortality." (Counsels on Health, 22). So, we can conclude that God's health program was given to assist us in attaining to fullness of life. Anyone who desires to experience this fullness of life should gladly embrace this provision.

However, there is widespread neglect, and sometimes rejection, of the health reform program that the Lord has provided for His church! Many people believe in the benefits of physical exercise but will not make the time to engage in it. "We need to remember that time spent in physical exercise is not lost... Physical inaction lessens not only mental but moral power." (Education, 208). Some know of the benefits of drinking adequate water but think they can't tolerate that much. When it comes to the diet aspect of the program, some believe that God's provision is inadequate for optimal health. If that were so, God would have made a mistake in Eden.

Ellen White has given us a comprehensive outline of God's health program, and science and personal experiences have attested to its benefits. Wherever church members have genuinely followed the program, they have been found to have a distinct advantage over the rest of the population. For those who have forgotten or are ignorant of it, here it is: "Pure air, sunlight, abstemiousness, rest, exercise, proper diet, the use of water, trust in divine power—these are the true remedies. Every person should have a knowledge of nature's remedial agencies and how to apply them" *(Ministry of Healing*, 127).

The Systematic Benevolence program is given to assist us in developing unselfish characters. No selfish person will enter the kingdom of God. Jesus teaches this very clearly in the parable of the sheep and goats in Matthew 25. Systematic Benevolence is the program that requires us to set aside a portion of our income to support the work of God and assist needy members of the human family. This practice was instituted in Old Testament times and continued in New Testament dispensation. All those who appreciate Jesus' great sacrifice to bring us salvation will gladly participate in this grand enterprise to rescue souls for God's kingdom. Ellen White endorses this notion:

"That man might not lose the blessed results of benevolence, our Redeemer formed the plan of enlisting him as His coworker. God could have reached His object in saving sinners without the aid of man; but He knew that man could not be happy without acting a part in the great work. By a chain of circumstances which would call forth his charities, He bestows upon man the best means of cultivating benevolence, and keeps him habitually giving to help the poor and to advance His cause. By its necessities a ruined world is drawing forth from us talents of means and of influence, to present to men and women the truth, of which they are in perishing need. And as we heed these calls, by labor and by acts of benevolence, we are assimilated to the image of Him who for our sakes became poor. In bestowing, we bless others, and thus accumulate true riches. It is the glory of the gospel that it is founded upon the principle of restoring in the fallen race the divine image by a constant manifestation of benevolence." CS 13

The program of Christian Education was given not just to make academically brilliant students but also to assist them in developing godly characters and being prepared to live with Christ forever. What sense would it make for our children to become brilliant academics and excellent professionals and then be excluded from heaven? Ellen White writes much about true education:

"The true object of education is to restore the image of God in the soul. In the beginning, God created man in His own likeness. He endowed him with noble qualities. His mind was well balanced, and all the powers of his being were harmonious. But the fall and its effects have perverted these gifts. Sin has marred and well-nigh obliterated the image of God in man. It was to restore this that the plan of salvation was devised, and a life of probation was granted to man. To bring him back to the perfection in which he was first created is the great object of life—the object that underlies every other. It is the work of parents and teachers, in the education of the youth, to cooperate with the divine purpose; and in so doing they are "laborers together with God." (*Patriarchs and Prophets*, 595).

Passionate, joyful witnessing characterizes the life of every true child of God. It is automatic. Once we are enjoying Jesus, we will have a burning desire to share Him with others. The Samaritan woman whom Jesus met at the well, having received the water of life from Jesus, went home and told everyone about Him, inviting them to come and experience Him for themselves. The Gadarene demoniac, after being healed by Jesus, was told to keep quiet about it. However, immediately after leaving, he began to publish it everywhere. As Ellen White explains, "When we share in God's work on earth, it prepares us to share in the joys of heaven, God could have reached His object in saving sinners without our aid; but in order for us to develop a character like Christ's, we must share in His work. In order to enter into His joy, —the joy of seeing souls redeemed by His sacrifice, —we must participate in His labours for their redemption." (*Desire of Ages* 142).

QUESTIONS FOR CONTEMPLATION

1. How important is health to life?
2. What is the purpose of the health message that the Lord has given to His people?
3. Where else in the Bible does God connect health with spirituality?
4. How does supporting God's work help in our spiritual development?
5. What advantage does Christian Education give our children?

6. What are some benefits of witnessing?

7. Are you presently practising the principles of God's health programme, if not, why?

Chapter 20

Those Who Will Hear The "Well Done"

The Christian life is a journey that will not end until, by God's grace, we set foot in the New Jerusalem. As this journey continues, we grow in grace, knowledge, wisdom, understanding, commitment, faith, and love. In other words, we become more and more like Jesus because Christlikeness is the goal. The Beloved Disciple, John, expresses it beautifully: "Beloved, now are we the sons of God, and it doth not yet appear what we shall be; but we know that when He shall appear, we shall be like Him, for we shall see Him as He is. And every man that has this hope in Him purifieth himself, even as He is pure." (1 John 3: 2-3). At no point on the journey can we say we have arrived. That will not be the case until we hear from the lips of our Saviour, "Well done, thou good and faithful servant; enter thou into the joy of Thy Lord" (Matthew 25).

This work of character development takes time and effort on our part. This is not salvation by works; it is cooperating with Christ. Ellen White expresses it well: "Sanctification is not the work of a moment, an hour, or a day. It is a continual growth in grace. We know not one day how strong our conflict will be the next. Satan lives, and is active, and every day we need to cry earnestly to God for help and strength to resist him. As long as Satan reigns we shall have self to subdue, besetment to overcome, and there is no stopping place, there is no point to which we can come and say we have fully attained" (*Counsels to the Church*, 51).

While salvation is by grace through faith, because Jesus purchased it with His blood, we still have a role to play in accepting it. Paul says that we are to work out our own salvation with fear and trembling, for it is God who works in us to will and to do of His good pleasure. (Philippians 2:12-13). Again, Ellen White explains, "The Christian life is constantly an onward march. Jesus sits as a refiner and purifier of His people; and when His image is perfectly reflected in them, they are perfect and holy, and prepared for translation" (Counsels to the Church 51). Also, she says that "Christ is waiting with longing desire for the manifestation of Himself in His church. When the character of

Christ shall be perfectly reproduced in His people, then He will come to claim them as His own" (*Christ's Object Lessons*, 69).

This endeavor might seem challenging and, to some, impossible, but as long as we keep trusting in Jesus and appreciating His love and mercy, we will overcome. Here is a blessed assurance from God's messenger: "Here is a course by which we may be assured that we shall never fall. Those who are thus working upon the plan of addition in obtaining the Christian graces have the assurance that God will work upon the plan of multiplication in granting them the gifts of His Spirit" (CCh 51). So, one day, all of God's people living on the earth at that time will reach this exalted state.

Though the church is feeble and defective now, that day will come when God's people finally experience the fullest expression of the abundant life that Jesus has promised. The Bible refers to this group of end-time believers that will achieve this significant milestone as the "'One Hundred and Forty-four Thousand." Here is how Revelation describes them: "

And I looked, and, lo, a Lamb stood on the mount Sion, and with him an hundred forty and four thousand, having his Father's name written in their foreheads. And I heard a voice from heaven, as the voice of many waters, and as the voice of a great thunder: and I heard the voice of harpers harping with their harps: And they sung as it were a new song before the throne, and before the four beasts, and the elders: and no man could learn that song but the hundred and forty and four thousand, which were redeemed from the earth. These are they which were not defiled with women; for they are virgins. These are they which follow the Lamb whithersoever he goeth. These were redeemed from among men, being the firstfruits unto God and to the Lamb. And in their mouth was found no guile: for they are without fault before the throne of God" (Revelation 14:1-5).

These are the people who will hear from the lips of Jesus the most pleasing words, "Well done," and will receive the most gracious invitation, "Come, ye blessed of my Father: inherit the kingdom prepared for you from the foundation of the world:" (*Matthew* 25:34). Having come through the Great Tribulation, they will have washed their robes and made them white in the blood of the Lamb (Revelation 7:14). They will live and reign with Christ and angels for one thousand years in heaven. They will attend the Marriage Supper of The Lamb (Revelation 19). After that, they will experience the joy of living on the New Earth forever.

Fellow pilgrims, we cannot afford to miss this grandest of all experiences! It is worth all the sacrifices we might be called upon to make! Heaven will be cheap enough! It will be worth it all when we see Jesus! On the other hand, what would it profit us if we gained the whole world and then missed heaven? (Mark 8:36)

God wants us there because He purchased it for us with the precious blood of His only Son. How could we escape if we neglect such a great salvation?

My family, my relatives, my brethren, my friends, do you want to be there? Are you planning and preparing to be there? I trust you do! We cannot afford otherwise to miss out! But let me remind you of the words of this song: "We speak of the realms of the blest, that country so bright and so fair; and oft all its glories confess; But what must it be to be there?"

If we are planning to be there, we must, by God's grace, begin to experience the abundant life that Jesus came to give us. We must from now begin to be filled with all the fullness of God, and "We need to keep ever before us this vision of things unseen. It is thus that we shall be able to set a right value on the things of eternity and the things of time.," (*Ministry of Healing*, 508)

Let us "stand on the threshold of eternity and hear the gracious welcome given to those who in this life have cooperated with Christ, regarding it as a privilege and an honor to suffer for His sake. With the angels, they cast their crowns at the feet of the redeemer, exclaiming, 'worthy is the lamb that was slain to receive power and riches and wisdom, and strength, and honor, and glory, and blessing'.... They unite in praising Hhim who died that human beings might have the life that measures with the life of God" (*Ibid*, 506).

BY GOD'S GRACE, LET US BE THERE!

QUESTIONS FOR CONTEMPLATION

1. Do you spend much time thinking about life in the New Earth?

2. Are you becoming a better Christian as we get nearer to the return of Jesus?

3. List some of the characteristics of the one hundred and forty-four thousand?

4. Give one reason why Jesus has not yet returned for His people?

5. Is there anything you can do to make Jesus come quicker?

About the Author

Pastor Astor Bowers is a second-generation Seventh-day Adventist. He is the only boy and the last of four children for his parents. Although he was born to non-Adventist parents, his mother left the Baptist Church and became a Seventh-day Adventist two years after his birth.

Against his father's angry objections, his mother carried him and his three sisters to church with her, and he was baptized at the age of thirteen. Though shy and reserved, he participated in several church programs and held many office positions, including Sabbath School and Missionary Volunteer Secretary, Missionary Volunteer Leader, and Church Leader.

He was educated in the public school system up to the secondary level and later taught as a pre-trained teacher at the primary level, though he never really wanted to become a teacher. However, he developed a liking for teaching and started planning to become a trained teacher, but the Lord miraculously intervened and changed his direction.

After spending four years as a successful teacher and planning to attend one of Jamaica's prominent teacher-training institutions, the Lord called him to pastoral ministry, so he enrolled at the then West Indies College in Mandeville, Jamaica. He graduated in 1981 and began working at West Jamaica Conference, where he spent thirty-three years serving as district pastor, departmental director, Executive Secretary, and Conference President. He was called to the Jamaica Union in 2014, where he served as ministerial secretary and stewardship director for four years. He accepted a call to the North Jamaica Conference in 2018 and served there for five years until he retired gracefully at the end of August. Though retired, he is still active in ministry, preaching, teaching, and conducting seminars. His favorite subjects are end-time prophecy and stewardship.

He is married to the former Winsome Ricketts and has two adult children. He has a master's degree in religion from Andrews University and a Doctor of Ministry from the Inter-American Adventist Theological Seminary.